AF488033

CULTURAL ANTHROPOLOGY

VENKATA MOHAN

XpressPublishing
An imprint of Notion Press

No.8, 3rd Cross Street,CIT Colony,
Mylapore, Chennai, Tamil Nadu-600004

ISBN 978-1-63633-163-8

Contents

Preface

The book introduces you to anthropology, covers research methods, gender-based issues, economic and political organisations and religion. It can serve as a good textbook for students of anthropology, while also helping sociology students.

The students will get a clear grasp of how various institutions of the society have evolved over a period of time and how these institutions are all interlinked. They will also know what their current status is and in which directions social change is taking place. The book gives many India-related examples.

Key technical terms are defined. The students are expected to answer the questions given at the end of each chapter to reinforce their understanding.

I hope this book helps students to look at our society in a more critical way.

Venkata Mohan
July 2020

CHAPTER ONE

Anthropology and Its Branches

1. Meaning and scope

Anthropology is a discipline that studies humans, focussing on the study of differences and similarities, both biological and cultural, in human populations. It is concerned with typical biological and cultural characteristics of human populations in all periods and in all parts of the world.

It is a study of human populations – similarities as well as differences. It is not confined to populations living today. It studies the past populations too. It is not confined to any one country, or any one continent. All the parts of the world are covered. It studies not simply the cultural aspects but biological as well.

It is a very wide field, as the name itself suggests. 'Anthropos' in Greek means man or human and 'logos' means study. Anthropology means the study of man. But the 'study of man' is too broad and lacks specificity. If anthropology intends to study man across time and space, how does it draw boundaries around itself? How does it make itself different from the other disciplines that study man?

Anthropologists tend to focus on the typical characteristics of human populations. They do not go into the social groups within a population, nor do they specialise in any one aspect of culture. Their study of a population is holistic. **Holistic** refers to an approach that studies many aspects of a multifaceted system. An anthropologist tends to ask what a population is in its essence. The population may be big or small, rich or poor, advanced or not advanced. He or she attempts to gain a broader understanding of a population and thereby of humankind. Details are used to build a bigger picture of man.

Traditionally, anthropology focussed on non-Western cultures. But nowadays anthropologists from the Western cultures are studying certain communities within their own societies.

2. Cultural anthropology

There are two broad divisions in anthropology: physical anthropology and cultural anthropology. Cultural anthropology is further divided into three subfields: archaeology, linguistics and ethnology. Archaeology studies the distant past whereas ethnology studies the recent past and present. Nowadays ethnology is usually referred to by its parent name cultural anthropology.

Ethnology is the study of how and why recent cultures differ and are similar. It is an analysis of cultures. **Ethnography** refers to a description of a society's customary behaviours and ideas. It contributes data to ethnology. Ethnography is produced by an ethnographer. An **ethnographer** is a person who spends some time living with, interviewing, and observing a group of people to describe their customs.

Many cultures have changed rapidly in the recent past. Through interviewing the present people, we would not know what their customs had been few years ago. Many societies changed due to contact with the dominant cultures. Ethnohistory helps in understanding these recent changes. An **ethnohistorian** is an ethnologist who uses historical documents to study how a particular culture has changed over time. While ethnographers provide the data by living with a group of people to study their culture, ethnohistorians provide the data by examining the accounts left by the missionaries, traders, explorers and government reports.

In ethnology, generalisations are important and cross-cultural research leads to generalisations. A **cross-cultural researcher** is an ethnologist who uses ethnographic data about many societies to test possible explanations of cultural variation to discover general patterns about cultural traits – what is universal, what is variable, why traits vary, and what the consequences of the variability might be. This is how cultural anthropology is generated.

3. *Biological anthropology*

Biological (physical) anthropology is the study of humans as biological organisms, dealing with the emergence and evolution of humans and with contemporary biological variations among human populations. It studies the physical or biological side of man – his past as well as his present, how he evolved as well as what he is now.

Physical anthropology includes **human paleontology (paleoanthropology)** which is the study of the emergence of humans and their later physical evolution. Human evolution is studied with the help of fossils. **Fossils** refer to the hardened remains or impressions of plants and animals that lived in the past.

Fossil evidence is interpreted to speculate what humans could have been like at one time and who were the ancestors to humans. Knowledge of earth sciences (geography and geology) is needed in this interpretation. The study of primates too plays an important role in interpreting the fossil evidence. A **primate** is a member of the mammalian order Primates, divided into the two suborders of prosimians and anthropoids. A **primatologist** is the one who studies primates.

Biological anthropology also involves the study of **human variation**, which is the study of how and why contemporary human populations vary biologically. Currently, all the people living on the earth belong to one and the same species,. That is **Homo sapines,** which means that all human populations on earth can successfully interbreed. The first Homo sapiens may have emerged about

200,000 years ago.

In the study of human variation, three disciplines are made use of – human genetics, population biology and epidemiology. Human genetics is the study of inherited human traits. Population biology is the study of environmental effects on, and interaction with, population characteristics. Epidemiology is the study of how and why diseases affect different populations in different ways.

4. Archaeology

Archaeology is the branch of anthropology that seeks to reconstruct the daily life and customs of peoples who lived in the past and to trace and explain cultural changes. Often lacking written records for study, archaeologists must try to reconstruct history from the material remains of human cultures.

Whereas ethnology is about the recent past or present, archaeology is about the distant past. Archaeology studies ancient cultures mostly with the help of material remains. How is archaeology different from the discipline of history? History is limited to the last 5000 years of human history and to the small proportion of societies that developed writing. Human societies existed for more than a million years, and archaeology attempts to study these societies of the distant past.

Archaeology deals with **prehistory**, which refers to the time before written records, but it also covers some societies that left written records. **Historical archaeology** is a speciality within archaeology that studies the material remains of recent peoples who left written records.

Archaeology asks questions such as where did tool-making emerge, where did agriculture develop and where did first cities emerge. To understand the cultures of the distant past, a knowledge of the present-day cultures is useful as a way of comparison. A knowledge of the earth sciences would also be useful to locate possible sites of significance as well as to help interpret the remains found at such sites.

5. *Anthropological linguistics*

Anthropological linguistics is the anthropological study of languages. **Linguistics** is the study of languages and is older than anthropology as a disicpline. But linguistics studies only the written languages of past and present. Linguistic anthropologists study the languages that are not written. They have to reconstruct their vocabulary and grammar.

Anthropological linguists study how languages differ from each other as well as how they evolved. **Descriptive linguistics**refers to the study of how languages are constructed. They study how sounds and words are put together.

Historical linguisticsrefers to the study of how languages change over time. Historical linguistics trace changes in languages over time and from what common language, different languages emerged.

Sociolinguisticsis the study of cultural and subcultural patterns of speaking in different social contexts. It studies the interface between society and language.

6. *Applied anthropology*

Applied anthropologyis the branch of anthropology that concerns itself with applying anthropological knowledge to achieve practical goals. Applied or **practicing anthropology** is the fifth field crosscutting the four fields of anthropology mentioned above – archaeology, linguistics, ethnology and biological anthropology.

For most of anthropology's history, anthropologists generally worked in academic institutions. But more and more of them are working outside academia in our times. Many of them are working in government agencies, international development agencies, private consulting firms, public health organisations, medical schools, law offices and charitable foundations.

Biological anthropologists may be called upon to give forensic evidence or in designing public health programs or in designing clothes and equipment to fit the human anatomy. Archaeologists are employed in managing museums or managing excavation sites. Anthropological linguists are called upon to help in bilingual educational training programs or in exploring ways to improve communication. Ethnologists may work in a wide variety of projects related to community development, urban planning or studies on the impact of cultural change. In a number of countries, anthropologists are being called upon to solve practical social problems.

7. Relationship with other disciplines

Cultural anthropology comes closest to sociology among all the social sciences. The difference between these two is that cultural anthropology focusses on simple cultures whereas sociology focuses on complex cultures. The methods they employ are also different. In cultural anthropology, field work is a very important method. In sociology, questionnaires and interviews are more important. Both the disciplines study societies holistically – economy, polity, religion, kinship – and seek to explore the interrelationships among the various aspects of the society.

Since cultural anthropology covers the contemporary too, though not as comprehensively as in sociology, its scope is much wider. Its data base is vast.

Cultural anthropology has been historically developed not only as the study of the simple societies, but also as the study of societies seen as 'the other'. An anthropologist leaves his own society to study another society. Sociology, however, involves the study of one's own society. But this differentiation could get complicated sometimes. M. N. Srinivas, for example, is seen as a sociologist in India, but is regarded as an anthropologist abroad, because he wrote about the rural India. Rural India, to the West, is an example of 'the other' while at the same time being a simple society.

Economics specialises in the economies of advanced societies. It has many theories and models on how economies run and how they should run. Economic anthropology is a part of cultural anthropology that focusses on the economies of simple societies. A lot is written on the similarities and differences between the economies of simple societies and complex societies and how far theories developed for complex economies are relevant to simple economies.

Political science specialises in the politics of advanced societies. It has theories on how power operates and how it should operate. Political anthropology is a part of cultural anthropology. It studies simple societies, compares how the political institutions there are different from those in complex societies. Political anthropology studies how political institutions are embedded in other aspects of culture.

Psychology focusses on the individual, not on the society or culture. But culture is shared by the individuals. Culture shapes the individuals. The individuals are socialised by their cultures. Anthropology also studies the interaction between the culture and the individual personality.

History's main focus is on the particulars – this place, this event, the relationship between the events. Cultural anthropology on the other hand seeks generalisation from the particulars. Also, whereas history studies the societies that have written records, cultural anthropology studies those without written records.

Anthropology is interdisciplinary. It draws heavily from sociology. It draws from political science for the political aspects of culture, from economics for the economic aspects, from psychology for the psychological aspects, from history to know the past, from linguistics to study the languages.

Earth sciences are also important in the process of uncovering and interpreting fossils – in the field of physical anthropology. Life sciences and medical sciences have an important place in charting human evolution and explaining human variation.

Terms

1. Anthropology: a discipline that studies humans, focussing on the study of differences and similarities, both biological and cultural, in human populations. It is concerned with typical biological and cultural characteristics of human populations in all periods and in all parts of the world.

2. Holistic: refers to an approach that studies many aspects of a multifaceted system.

3. Biological (physical) anthropology: the study of humans as biological organisms, dealing with the emergence and evolution of humans and with contemporary biological variations among human populations.

4. Cultural anthropology: the study of cultural variation and universals in the past and present.

5. Applied anthropology: the branch of anthropology that concerns itself with applying anthropological knowledge to achieve practical goals.

6. Human paleontology (paleoanthropology): the study of the emergence of humans and their later physical evolution.

7. Human variation: the study of how and why contemporary human populations vary biologically.

8. Fossils:the hardened remains or impressions of plants and animals that lived in the past.

9. Primate:a member of the mammalian order Primates, divided into the two suborders of prosimians and anthropoids.

10. Primatologists: People who study primates.

11. Homo sapiens: All living people belong to one biological species, Homo sapiens, which means that all human populations on earth can successfully interbreed. The first Homo sapiens may have emerged about 200,000 years ago.

12. Ethnology: the study of how and why recent cultures differ and are similar.

13. Ethnographer:a person who spends some time living with, interviewing, and observing a group of people to describe their customs.

14. Ethnography:a description of a society's customary behaviours and ideas.

15. Ethnohistorian:an ethnologist who uses historical documents to study how a particular culture has changed over time.

16. Cross-cultural researcher: An ethnologist who uses ethnographic data about many societies to test possible explanations of cultural variation to discover general patterns about cultural traits – what is universal, what is variable, why traits vary, and what the consequences of the variability might be.

17. Archaeology:the branch of anthropology that seeks to reconstruct the daily life and customs of peoples who lived in the past and to trace and explain cultural changes. Often lacking written records for study, archaeologists must try to reconstruct history from the material remains of human cultures.

18. Prehistory the time before written records.

19. Historical archaeology: a speciality within archaeology that studies the material remains of recent peoples who left written records.

20. Anthropological linguistics:the anthropological study of languages.

21. Linguistics:the study of languages.

22. Descriptive (structural) linguistics:the study of how languages are constructed.

23. Historical linguistics:the study of how languages change over time.

24. Sociolinguistics: the study of cultural and subcultural patterns of speaking in different social contexts.

Think on it

1. Define anthropology.
2. What is the scope of anthropology?
3. What is the focus of anthropology?
4. What is meant by holistic study?

5. Does anthropology exclude Western cultures?

6. What is ethnology?

7. Is ethnology being equated with cultural anthropology?

8. How is ethnography different from ethnology?

9. How is an ethnographer different from ethnohistorian?

10. Who is a cross-cultural researcher?

11. What is the scope of physical anthropology?

12. What is paleoanthropology?

13. What are fossils?

14. Who is a primate?

15. When did Homo sapiens emerge?

16. What does population genetics study?

17. What does population biology study?

18. What is epidemiology?

19. Define archaeology as a branch of anthropology.

20. What is the scope of archaeology?

21. How is prehistory different from historical archaeology?

22. What is the scope of anthropological linguistics?

23. How is descriptive linguistics different from historical linguistics?

24. What is sociolinguistics?

25. What is applied anthropology?

26. Discuss in what fields anthropologists can be employed outside academic institutions.

27. Discuss the relationship of anthropology with other disciplines.

CHAPTER TWO

Culture and Society

The concepts of culture and society are central to cultural anthropology. Take the word 'culture'. Anthropology uses this word differently from some types of common usage. Some students may think culture is a reference to art, drama, music, sculpture or architecture. But they are only a part of culture, and culture means a lot more than that in anthropology. Some may think if people behave in a refined and sophisticated way, then they have culture. But that is also not the way the word is used in anthropology.

Culture in anthropology refers to the total way of life. Every man – rich or poor, educated or not – participates in culture. There is no one without culture. **Culture** refers to the set of learned behaviours and ideas (including beliefs, attitudes, values and ideals) that are characteristic of a particular society or other social group.

Culture is everything, everything that is learned by a society or a group. Culture is everything of what is learned. Hair style is a part of culture, hair colour is not. Eating habits are a part of culture, not the fact that we eat. Culture refers only to what is learnt and not biologically inherited.

Culture includes various aspects – be it political, economic or technological. Computers too are a part of culture. Democracy, family system, cities, slums and villages and factories are all a part of culture. Schools and textbooks, the rates of illiteracy, the rates of suicides as well as the number of murders are all aspects of culture.

The concept of culture is closely linked to the concept of society. If a culture refers to a lifestyle, it is a society that has that lifestyle.

It is a society that has a culture. **Society**refers to a group of people who occupy a particular territory and speak a common language not generally understood by neighbouring peoples. By this definition, societies do not necessarily correspond to countries.

The concept of society as defined here refers to people who occupy a territory and who have a common culture. One evidence for a common culture is a common language. And how do we know where one society ends and where a new one begins? It is where the language spoken in one territory is not understood by the people of a neighbouring territory. These two societies have different cultures. This is how cultural anthropology regards a society. A country is not a society. India has many societies within it. It has many populations speaking different languages.

A society's distinct way of life is its culture. If one society has some features that another society also has, then there are cultural similarities between these two societies.

A society has a culture, but some groups within a society may have somewhat distinct cultures, these cultures are called subcultures. **Subculture** refers to the shared customs of a subgroup within a society. The poor people, for example, may have a particular culture which can be called the culture of poverty.

Culture is something that is shared in the society. We can say the defining features of a culture are: 1) it is learned and 2) it is shared. If it is not shared, it is not a culture at all.

Culture is distinguished from civilisation. **Civilisation**is the culture of an urban society. In India, civilisation started with the Indus Valley civilisation. Societies that have not evolved to have cities are not considered civilised. People at a hunting-gathering stage have their distinct culture, but they are not civilised. A civilisation has towns, it has various specialists, it has a hierarchy of political officers, a king or a council and an army. Civilisation can be taken as an advanced stage in culture. People during the Neolithic period and the Paleolithic period are said to have cultures, they did not belong to civilisations.

Some scholars like the American sociologist MacIver differentiate between culture and civilisation in a different way. Culture is regarded by them as the sum total of moral, spiritual and intellectual attainments of man. It stands for symbols and values. It is inside us. In this view, civilisation is taken to be technology and wealth that form the material aspects of a society. It is outside us. If used in this sense, one can argue that while civilisation is improving, culture may not be. This kind of distinction, however, is not made in cultural anthropology nowadays.

Anthropologists study how cultures change, how they evolve. Anthropologists normally belong to technologically advanced countries and they typically study societies with a very simple level of technology. Anthropology specialises in the study of simple societies.

One principle anthropologists try to follow in their study of other cultures is that they do not judge other cultures on the basis of the norms followed in their own societies. **Norms**refer to standards or rules about what is acceptable behaviour. An anthropologist will not judge polyandry in a society as immoral because his society considers it immoral. He will not judge premarital sex as bad because his society considers it so. He is trained not to be ethnocentric.

Ethnocentrismrefers to the attitude that other societies' customs and ideas can be judged in the context of one's own culture. An anthropologist is trained to be free from ethnocentrism. He is supposed to believe in cultural relativism. **Cultural relativism**refers to the attitude that a society's customs and ideas should be viewed within the context of that society's problems and opportunities.

If a society is following polyandry, why is it doing so? What are the environmental or technological factors that contribute to polyandry? An anthropologist is supposed to investigate it that way. That is cultural relativism. Cultural relativism is the opposite of ethnocentrism.

Why can't an anthropologist evaluate polyandry in terms of his own society's values? Why should polyandry be understood in terms of the factors of that particular society to which it belongs? Because an anthropologist believes that cultural traits are interrelated; one trait is related to another trait, and all the traits seen in a society put together may be contributing to the survival of that society.

However, an anthropologist does not assume that every trait seen in a society must be adaptive in nature. He may consider some traits adaptive and some maladaptive. **Adaptive customs** refer to cultural traits that enhance survival and reproductive success in a particular environment. **Maladaptive customs** refer to cultural traits that diminish the chances of survival and reproduction in a particular environment.

Cultural traits are interlinked, a culture is patterned but the pattern is not perfect. That is why maladaptive customs continue. The customs that were once adaptive may continue even after becoming maladaptive. Also, following one custom might mean violating another custom. A culture is normally imperfectly patterned.

Cultural relativism does not mean absence of judgement. It only means not judging on the basis of the values of one's own culture. A cultural trait can be judged on some other basis which is valid. Some cultural traits can be judged on certain universal criteria of human rights. An anthropologist can also propose a planned intervention to modify or remove a particular cultural trait.

Cultures change and they change due to certain internal factors or because of influences by other cultures. **Diffusion** refers to the process by which cultural elements are borrowed from another society and incorporated into the culture of the recipient group. Many elements of culture in any society can be usually traced to the elements in very distant societies. This is because of diffusion of cultural traits.

Much cultural change in simple societies takes place in the context of a superior-subordinate relationship with complex societies. When a European country colonises a particular territory, they colonise many societies living on that territory. Sweeping changes are introduced in those societies. The colonial powers may force change by introducing new laws, or by converting the people to their religion or by introducing their education system. Colonialism leads to the resource erosion of the colonised – lands taken, forests occupied. The people living there may no longer be able to follow their traditional cultures.

These kinds of cultural changes are covered under acculturation. **Acculturation**refers to the process of extensive borrowing of aspects of culture in the context of superior-subordinate relations between societies; usually occurs as a result of external pressure. Colonialism led to massive changes across many societies. Some simple societies did not have the time to acculturate themselves, they simply died out due to new diseases brought by the colonisers.

J. Herskovits says when a growing child learns to conform to his own culture, that is **enculturation**. When there is an exchange of cultural traits between different societies, it is **transculturation**. When one way of life is being displaced by another, it is acculturation. But when the dominated culture tries to recover and begins to assert its identity, it is called **contra-acculturation**.

Currently, globalisation is the force behind change in many societies. **Globalisation**refers to the ongoing spread of goods, people, information and capital around the world. It causes diffusion of certain cultural traits.

Does globalisation lead to a loss of cultural diversity? Not necessarily. Societies want to maintain their distinct identities, they will not lose their culture easily. Cultural diversity may not disappear entirely though similarities across cultures keep increasing.

Non-human culture

Jane Goodall studied chimpanzees in the Gombe National Park in Tanzania. She discovered that chimps fish for ants and termites.

Fishing for ants involves firstly breaking off a twig, then stripping it of leaves and side branches, and then locating a suitable termite nest and inserting the twig. The termites inside cling to the twig, the chimp pulls it out and licks off the termites clinging to it. (Goodall, 1986).

Young chimps learn this technique through trial and error. At about 18 to 22 months, they begin to fish for termites on their own. They become efficient when they are about 3 years old. Ants that can inflict a painful bite are also fished similarly. But it takes one year more for the chimps to master the technique.

This phenomenon of anting is a cultural phenomenon. How do we know that anting is cultural? Though ants and chimps are there in other places in Africa, those ants are not eaten by the chimps. At certain other places, anting is done but it is done differently.

Chimps can also make a 'sponge' for sopping up water from inaccessible parts of a tree. They strip a handful of leaves, put them in the mouth and chew briefly, and put that mass of leaves in the water, let them soak, then they put the damp mass of leaves in their mouths and suck the water off.

Chimps also use sticks for digging purpose.

Chimps of Tai forest of Ivory Coast open the hard shells of the panda nut with rocks that serve as hammers. They search for suitable hammer stone and bring them from distance for this purpose.

The cultures seen among the non-human species are at very rudimentary level. And these cultures do not evolve. Nevertheless, they are cultures because they have behavioural traits that are learnt as well as shared.

Social groups

No society is simply a collection of individuals, the individuals exist as members of social groups in a society. **Social group**refers to a collection of individuals who interact in systematic ways with one another. Groups may range from very small associations to large-scale organisations or societies. It is a defining feature of a group, whatever its size, that its members have an awareness of a common identity. A family is a social group. A clan is a one. A caste is one.

All social groups need not be equal. Some societies are stratified and there are inequalities across groups. **Social stratification**refers to presence of social groups such as families, classes, or ethnic groups that have unequal access to important advantages such as economic resources, power and prestige.

As members of a society or a social group, individuals are expected to behave in a particular way. **Social role**refers to the expected behaviour of an individual occupying a particular social position. Each role has certain norms associated with it. In every society, individuals play a number of different social roles. Social role corresponds to a position in the society, that position is also called status. When a man and a woman marry, they become 'husband' and 'wife'. They attain the status of husband and the status of wife. When they have children, they attain the statuses of 'father' and 'mother'. Statuses of individuals change, their social roles change correspondingly .

Statuses like these – a husband, a father – are called ascribed statuses. **Ascribed status** refers to what is assigned without reference to the innate differences or abilities. Ascribed status is different from achieved status. If one becomes the headman of a band, that is an achieved status. **Achieved status**is acquired through talent, efforts and accomplishments, rather than ascription. For example, a person has to pass exams to be a doctor in our society.

A social institution consists of persons with certain statuses and roles. Family as in institution has people with the social statuses of father, mother, brother, sister, son and daughter. They are expected to behave in a particular way – as per their social roles. These behavioral patterns are norms. The institution of a university creates the positions of director, professors, office staff and students. Society consists of social institutions. **Social structure** refers to patterns of interaction between individuals, groups and institutions. Most of our activities are structured: they are organised in a regular and repetitive way.

Terms

1. Culture: the set of learned behaviours and ideas (including beliefs, attitudes, values and ideals) that are characteristic of a particular society or other social group.

2. Society: a group of people who occupy a particular territory and speak a common language not generally understood by neighbouring peoples. By this definition, societies do not necessarily correspond to countries.

3. Subculture: the shared customs of a subgroup within a society.

4. Norms: standards or rules about what is acceptable behaviour.

5. Ethnocentrism: the attitude that other societies' customs and ideas can be judged in the context of one's own culture.

6. Cultural relativism: the attitude that a society's customs and ideas should be viewed within the context of that society's problems and opportunities.

7. Maladaptive customs: cultural traits that diminish the chances of survival and reproduction in a particular environment.

8. Adaptive customs: cultural traits that enhance survival and reproductive success in a particular environment.

9. Diffusion: the process by which cultural elements are borrowed from another society and incorporated into the culture of the recipient group.

10. Acculturation: the process of extensive borrowing of aspects of culture in the context of superior-subordinate relations between societies; usually occurs as a result of external pressure.

11. Globalisation: the ongoing spread of goods, people, information and capital around the world.

12. Social group: a collection of individuals who interact in systematic ways with one another. Groups may range from very small associations to large-scale organisations or societies. It is a defining feature of a group, whatever its size, that its members have an awareness of a common identity.

13. Social role: the expected behaviour of an individual occupying a particular social position. In every society, individuals play a number of different social roles, according to the varying contexts of their activities.

14. Social stratification: presence of social groups such as families, classes, or ethnic groups that have unequal access to important advantages such as economic resources, power and prestige.

15. Achieved status is acquired through talent, efforts and accomplishments, rather than ascription.

16. Ascribed status refers to what is assigned without reference to the innate differences or abilities.

17. Social structure refers to patterns of interaction between individuals, groups and institutions. Most of our activities are structured: they are organised in a regular and repetitive way.

Think on it

1. Define culture.

2. How is the concept of culture related to the concept of society?

3. What is a subculture?

4. What is the difference between culture and civilisation?

5. Are some populations uncivilised? Are they uncultured?

6. What is the difference between culture and civilisation?

7. List the features of a civilisation.

8. Can civilisation be equated with material culture?

9. What are norms?

10. What is ethnocentrism?

11. Why should not an anthropologist be ethnocentric?

12. What is cultural relativism?

13. Can we take cultural relativism as a foundational principle in anthropology? Explain.

14. Are all customs adaptive in a culture?

15. Why is culture patterned?

16. What is meant by imperfect pattern of a culture?

17. Does cultural relativism oppose intervention in a culture?

18. Can there be universal values by which cultures can be judged?

19. Should cultures be changed on the basis of certain universal values?

20. What is meant by diffusion?

21. How is acculturation different from diffusion?

22. Explain the processes behind acculturation.

23. What is globalisation?

24. What do you see is the future for cultural diversity in the world?

25. Is culture unique to humans? Explain.

26. Give examples of culture among chimps.

27. What is unique to human culture?

28. What is a social group?

29. What is social stratification?

30. What is the link between status and role?

31. What is a social institution? Give examples.

32. What is the difference between ascribed status and achieved status?

33. What is social structure?

CHAPTER THREE

Linguistic Anthropology

1. Historical linguistics

Anthropology tries to trace the origins of people. Here language plays a very important role and we study the origins of people through languages in the field of historical linguistics. Historical linguistics is the study of how languages change over time. Through the similarities in languages across populations, their connections in the remote past can be deduced. We can learn about their origins.

Irawati Karve studied the North Indian and the South Indian kinship systems. She could classify the kinship systems on the basis of languages. Similarities in language mean similarities in culture and society. How do we know that some societies were related to each other in the recent or remote past? It's often through the study of the languages. How do we know some societies are not at all related to each other? It is when they speak two languages that have absolutely no similarities.

How do we know from where the Aryans came to India? It's through the study of the languages. The language that the Aryans spoke belongs to the Indo-European family of languages. There would have been a Proto-Indo-European language, PIE, that was the origin of all Indo-European languages. A **protolanguage**refers to a hypothesised ancestral language from which two or more languages seem to have derived. And from this Proto-Indo-European language, Sanskrit emerged as well as well as Greek, Latin and other languages. That's why we have common words between Indian and European languages. And tracing the origins through the study of a large number of these languages, linguists surmised that this Proto-Indo-European language was spoken by a group of people who lived in and around the Ukraine region in Europe.

Some gods of the Iranians are the same as the gods in India. For example, the god Yama. This could imply that some people from the same group migrated to Iran while some others came to India. Before migration, they had the same gods.

Language is a powerful tool to trace the ancestry of a group. It is useful to find out which language came from what source language and how the dialects developed. Often, dialects grow into full-fledged languages. A **dialect** refers to a variety of a language spoken in a particular area or by a particular social group. Over time,these dialects evolve. That's how one Proto-Indo-European language could give rise to many European languages as well as Sanskrit. And then from Sanskrit, many other Indian languages emerged, languages such as Gujarati, Marathi, Sindhi, and Hindi. They all have a common source. But Tamil is so completely different from the North Indian languages. Differences across language groups suggest differences in their origins.

2. *Origins of language*

Anthropologists also study the origins of speech in the human species. They think that some kind of rudimentary language existed even in the Neanderthal times. A particular gene, FOXP2, associated with language in the Homo sapiens was found in Neanderthals. The faculty of speech is an expression of higher cognitive functionality, which must be a result of the interactions of many genes. Symbolic art existed during the Upper Paleolithic. Written tablets date back to the dawn of civilisation.

While humans have a higher capacity for speech and language, communication itself did not start with humans. Communication systems exist even among animals. Monkeys have them, apes have them, as well as bees, dogs, cats and various other animals. Various animal species have their own communication systems. Complex communication systems have evolved through smells, sounds, dances and other bodily movements. Language is simply a more advanced system of communication, but a lot of culture could develop because of language. Much of culture could be communicated through language and passed down the generations.

Language is a part of vocal communication. Many things are also communicated through nonvocal means. **Kinesics** is the study of communication by nonvocal means, including posture, mannerisms, body movement, facial expressions, and signs and gestures. There is a cultural specificity as well as universality in human nonvocal communication. Expressions of fear, disgust and sadness are recognised across the various cultures. However, many aspects of nonverbal behaviour – gestures like nodding the head up and down or distance maintained between two persons – are culture-specific.

All vocal communication cannot be equated with verbal communication. Grunts, laughs, giggles, moans are vocal communication but are not verbal. **Paralanguage** refers to all the optional vocal features or silences apart from the language itself that communicate meaning.

For a long time, there was only oral communication among human beings. No written communication existed. One had to memorise things like poems and stories to tell them to others. There would be some distortions as the stories passed from person to another, down the generations. Then came writing. Societies became literate, and there was a huge explosion of learning, which is culture. Much of our culture is transmitted from one generation to the next through the written word. Language, both spoken and written, is the most important reason for the continuity of our culture as well as its advancement. We just cannot think of this kind of cultural advancement without language.

Anthropologists also study how languages are born and evolve. They think that there is an inherent pattern in the human mind that thinks in particular ways. The human mind has some innate language-learning capability. There was a debate in linguistics on whether a language is completely learnt or there already are predetermined structures. Noam Chomsky said that there are predetermined structures in the human mind, generating and experimenting with languages. Many anthropologists also believe that.

Anthropologists studied what are called pidgin and creole languages. A pidgin language develops when, for example, the colonial people brought slaves from different societies together. In America and other countries, slaves were brought in from different societies because it was easier to control them that way. The slaves did not know each other's language, nor did they know the European languages. But they came into forced interaction with one another and their masters. What did they do?

They spoke with their masters and among themselves in a new language. Anthropologists have studied this language. It is called a pidgin language. A pidgin language has extremely limited vocabulary, it lacks many building blocks of a language such as prepositions and auxiliary verbs. Many of these words came from the masters' language, but there were also words from the slaves' native languages, and a completely different grammar evolved. A pidgin language is the beginning of a new language, it starts in a very crude form. But what happens by the time the second and third generations are speaking this language? It becomes a creole language, it picks up a particular grammatical structure and becomes more refined.

Creole languages arose in many places in the world. Anthropologists found thattheys have a particular structure. Anthropologists study the structure of a language, how the sounds are made, how the grammar is derived, how sentences are formed and things like that. In the case of creole languages, they noticed that they have particular patterns. Derek Bickerton (1983) argues that striking similarities across creole languages go to prove some pattern is inherited by all humans.

Anthropologists also study how children learn language – how children pick up words and sentences and what kind of experiments they make with using words. Bickerton says the errors that children make are consistent with the grammar of the creole languages. This shows that there is some inherent predisposition in the human mind to develop language in certain ways. Various languages of the world developed along the possibilities that this inherent structure in the human mind makes possible.

Creole languages show how complex languages evolved from simple languages. We can't study the evolution of the language from the study of the language of the simple societies, because their language is not simple at all. Contrary to what people generally think, technologically primitive people do not have simple languages and technologically advanced people do not have more complex languages. Complexity in language evolved a long ago. People of primitive societies also have all the words they need to express a wide variety of things and their grammar is not simple. And then more importantly, whatever words they need to learn they can easily learn. A Chenchu will have his own vocabulary, but he can also learn other vocabularies. In that sense, the Chenchu language is not primitive.

Eskimos have many words for ice and snow, because they have to deal with them more closely than us. A modern person will have difficulty in recognising one type of snow from another type. In modern societies, a doctor will have huge separate vocabulary of his own profession, and it's the same with an engineer.

3. *Language and culture*

Another aspect of linguistic anthropology is the study of the interface between the society and the language. The society influences its language and the language influences the society by influencing thinking. Linguists Edward Sapir and Benjamin Lee Whorf suggested that language affects how individuals in a society perceive reality. If the social structure is hierarchical, there will be a plural 'you' to denote respect, as in Hindi "aap," for example. The words predispose the people to think as well as behave in a particular way. Another example would be how kin terms influence the way one views the kin. A society is viewed through its language by its people. People think about their society through the words they have. Language is shaped by the society and in it turn shapes the society.

What can we learn about a society from the study of its language? This is an important issue in linguistic anthropology. For example, in the context of Telangana vs Andhra, whose language was made a standard one in the undivided Andhra Pradesh? It was the Andhra language. In Telugu movies, the heroes speak the Andhra language, the villains tend to speak the Telangana language. What does it show? It shows the power equation.

You can see the caste differences in the usage of language. The language that the lower castes speak is different from the language that the higher castes speak. This shows that there is no free interaction between the people of various castes. And so far as there is any interaction, it is a power-related interaction. The language of the upper castes would be taken as the standard language. In this way, the study of dialects and accents can throw light on the social structure.

Which language is more respected in a multilingual society says something about that society. What is the role of English in the Indian society? English is a source of power. In a society like ours, people will have a problem with finding a job if they don't know English. If they know English, there is a greater chance of them getting a job. English is highly favored. Even if a person doesn't know anything else, just fluency or knowledge in the English language can enable his livelihood.

How about the relation among the languages in India? Are some languages preferred over others? Take Hindi vs the regional languages. People who speak Hindi don't think they need to learn English at all. They can confidently manage things just with Hindi. But the South Indian people who don't speak Hindi will have a difficulty. The North Indians make the South Indians feel it is their mistake if they don't know Hindi. South Indians are expected to learn Hindi. For the North Indians, they are supposed to know only Hindi. That leads to different confidence levels and different performances. Tamil Nadu went for anti-Hindi movement because it is opposed to this domination by the North Indians.

How some words are coined and used can reveal political processes. Who is a terrorist as opposed to a freedom fighter? Which terms imply bad things? How do certain words assume lot of emotional salience? Things like this can explain how knowledge, through language, is shaped by power.

In a country with multiple languages, people may switch from one language to another language – in the middle of a conversation or even in the middle of a sentence. This is called **code switching** –using more than one language in the course of conversing – and it follows a pattern. Mother tongue may be preferred for intimate conversation, English may be used to convey ideas. Status differences among the speakers, along with the extent of familiarity with the languages, will also determine which language may be spoken and for how long. In India, speaking in English gets higher status – next followed by Hindi.

Terms

1.**Protolanguage**: a hypothesised ancestral language from which two or more languages seem to have derived.

2. **Dialects:** a variety of a language spoken in a particular area or by a particular social group.

3. **Kinesics:** the study of communication by nonvocal means, including posture, mannerisms, body movement, facial expressions, and signs and gestures.

4. **Paralanguage:** refers to all the optional vocal features or silences apart from the language itself that communicate meaning.

5. **Accents:** differences in pronunciation characteristic of a group.

6. Symbolic communication: an arbitrary (not obviously meaningful) gesture, call, word or sentence that has meaning even when its referent is not present.

7. Core vocabulary: Nonspecialist vocabulary.

8. Code switching: Using more than one language in the course of conversing.

Think on it

1. What is meant by historical linguistics?

2. How is historical linguistics useful to trace origins and migrations of populations?

3. What is a protolanguage?

4. How is a language different from a dialect? What is an accent?

5. What is kinesics?

6. What is paralanguage?

7. In the course of human evolution, when did language speaking ability develop?

8.What is Chomsky's theory of language development?

9. What is a creole language? How is it different from a pidgin language?

10. Do simple societies speak simple languages? Explain.

11. Does language shape thinking? Explain.

12. Does social structure influence standardisation of language?

13. In a multi-lingual society, will some languages have advantage over others?

14. Can social hierarchy be studied through language?

CHAPTER FOUR

Research Methods

1. Methodology, method, technique

The research methods we are going to discuss are based on certain theories. Some of these methods could look somewhat obvious, but you need to know what theoretical issues are related to these methods.

Let us first clarify certain terms, starting with 'methodology'. Haralambos and Holborn use '**methodology**' to mean a broader framework of study. There are two frameworks, quantitative approach vs qualitative approach is what methodology is about. Those who believe that the methods of physical sciences also work in anthropology are called positivists. Those who do not believe so are called non-positivists. Positivists prefer a quantitative approach, non-positivists prefer a qualitative approach. The type of approach determines the methodology. Be clear when you use the word 'methodology', it is about the theoretical underpinning of your research.

The methodology comes from a **theoretical orientation**– which is a general attitude about how phenomena are to be explained. A theoretical orientation refers to more than any specific theory. Evolutionism is a theoretical orientation, but Tylor's theory of evolution of religion is a specific theory.

A **theory**is an explanation of associations. An **explanation**is an answer to a why question. What is an association? **Statistical association**or a **law**refers to correlation between two or more variables that is unlikely to be due to chance. A **variable**is a thing or quantity that varies. In F=ma, 'F', 'm' and 'a' are variables, and Newton's law is the statistical association among these three variables. A theory is the 'why' of this relationship which makes sense of it. A theory is much more than a statistical association.

From a certain methodology, certain **methods**arise. Questionnaire is a method. Interview is a method. Genealogy is a method. The way a method should be carried out is called a **technique**. The methodology is a broad thing, next comes the method, and then comes the technique, which is a smaller, more practical issue. A technique of interview is a smaller thing compared to a method of interview. But why you choose the interview method is a methodological issue.

2. Questionnaire

The quantitative approach involves a lot of data. It is statistical in nature, and involves analysing and arriving at conclusions. It requires a large sample. In contrast, the qualitative approach goes in-depth and is more insightful. Quantitative is about volume, qualitative is about depth. How we should study a phenomenon is a very important methodological issue. Should we go quantitatively or qualitatively? This is a very important decision that a researcher has to make.

Quantitative analysisis analysis based on precise measurement. **Qualitative analysis** deals with information that is not quantified. A survey is a part of quantitative analysis. A **survey**is a systematic gathering of information about a large number of individuals and their communities using oral and written questioning, administering tools such as questionnaire and interview schedules and then interpreting the data by applying statistical methods.

A **questionnaire** is a survey tool consisting of a set of questions which is self-administered by the respondent. An interviewer-completed instrument is known as interview schedule. **Interview** is a method of data collection where information is gathered through oral questioning.

An **interview schedule** in terms of its structure is a schedule identical to a questionnaire, but in this, the interviewer asks the questions and notes down the respondent's answers verbatim. A questionnaire, in contrast, is self-administered by the respondent.

An in-depth interview is an intensive, long-term, less structured interview in field work, which requires many sessions for completion. It stands in contrast to the structured interviews of survey research. In-depth interviews are used in qualitative analysis.

A questionnaire can either have closed-ended questions or open-ended questions. **Closed-ended questions,** also known as 'forced-choice', 'fixed-response', and 'fixed-choice' questions, limit (or force) the respondent to choose responses from the categories already provided. **Open-ended questions,** also termed 'free-response questions', do not have response options, instead give sufficient space to write (or dictate) his/her answer to the question. A **respondent** is the person who answers questions in an interview session or in a survey.

What are the advantages with closed-ended questions? They are easy to administer and easy to analyse. What is important is simply setting the right kind of questions and answer options. What are the right kind of questions? The researcher should think about what is it that needs to be known. Let's say, we want to know about the general attitude towards Muslims in the society. If we ask a question that is too direct like "Do you hate Muslims?" – people are not likely to admit that they hate, even if they do. So the researcher asks questions like, "Will you accept a Muslim as a neighbour?" That's a general question. "If your friend or friend's son is going to marry a Muslim woman, will you approve of it?" That's a more serious question. "If there is a rioting in the town, who will you think is more likely to be behind it – Hindus or Muslims?"

This is what is called, technically, operationalising the concept. **Operational definition**means measurement of concept, which implies the empirical measurement of a verbal concept. If a concept is not amenable to empirical measurement, it is not operational. You want to measure hatred, you want to measure prejudice or discrimination. You have to reduce a concept to a set of questions, the 'yes' and 'no' answers -- which will measure the extent of the prejudice. One can measure the level of acceptance of Muslims from the answers to a variety of questions. This measurement can be given on a scale that ranges from 'strongly approve' to 'strongly disapprove.'

You should have a deeper understanding of what you want to study. You should know how these prejudices could be reflected in the answers. You have to measure the prejudice of the respondent only from the responses given. That's how a questionnaire should be designed.

Reliability indicates the extent to which repeated measurements under the same conditions produce the same, consistent results. **Validity**indicates where the findings are in agreement with theoretical or conceptual values. A questionnaire has to be finally administered in such a way that it is both reliable and valid.

For something to be valid, it should first be reliable, but reliability may not be sufficient for validity. If a survey has to be reliable, the results should be the same regardless of the people who conduct the survey. If the people change the operational definitions, if they change the methods, then the results can be different. This issue is not of reliability but validity. Reliability is the replicability, given the same methods. Research methods should be both reliable and valid.

3. Case study

A case studyis an in-depth and comprehensive study of a social unit – be that unit a person, a group, a social institution, a district, a community or a society. This is a part of the qualitative approach.

If a person wants to study something like depression, which approach would be better: to study a few people suffering from depression in depth or to take a statistical survey on depression from a large group of people? Are the respondents likely to convey how exactly they feel or felt? How will we know what it is to be depressed? A respondent might say he feels lonely, but will that tell the researcher that this is depression?

Think, why a movie on a subject is more impressive than a newspaper article on that same subject? If it is just about the visual thing, we can get all the visual statistics on a TV channel. Would it be as impressive as a movie?

What moves you more – the death of a single person you know closely or the fact that a thousand people died somewhere? It is the death of the one person you know, because you are connected to him or her. Statistics don't touch us as much. A movie is more touching because in a movie you get to know so many personal things, it focusses on a single person or a few persons. Sometimes, a movie may be able to educate you more than any amount of statistics. Have you watched the Tamil movie 'Super Deluxe'? Is it not much more illuminating than any write-up on transgenders? Because you actually see what the life of a transgender person is. Can one set questions on transgenders without knowing what their life is like? Can you pose a transgender a question like "What will you think about your son? What experience did he face?" It is not possible.

When a researcher is from a different background and he wants to study about transgender people, he wouldn't know how to approach the subject. He therefore has to spend time learning about his subject, talking with people, discussing, travelling with them, only then can he know. The basic problem with designing a questionnaire is that the researcher should know what to ask. But he will know what to ask only when he already knows a lot about what he is studying. How else can he ask?

In an elite international school, some children were asked to write an essay on the life of a poor man. A boy wrote, "I know a poor family. In that family, everyone is poor. The father is poor, the cook is poor, the driver is poor, the security guard is poor!" That is the boy's notion of poverty. If the topic of his study is distant, a researcher may not be able to ask relevant questions. The questionnaire becomes less valid or invalid.

In the early days of anthropology, researchers used to send questionnaires to distant groups of people through missionaries and government officials. The anthropologists had no idea how these simple societies would be. They had only some vague notions and they were asking their questions based on them. Later they realised that the questionnaire method was wrong, because they just did not know what questions to ask. A questionnaire is based on the assumption that the researcher knows about the things generally but needs more data on the subject.

Participant observationrefers to living among the people being studied – observing, questioning and (when possible) taking part in the important events of the group; writing or otherwise recording notes on observations, questions asked and answered, and things to check out later are parts of participant – observation. This is part of **field work**, which is a first-hand experience with the people being studied and the usual means by which anthropological information is being obtained.

The tradition of participant observation started with Malinowski, who was forced to stay on an island near New Guinea during World War I. When he was living among the people there, he understood the limitations of the questionnaire method. The assumption behind a questionnaire is that researcher knows what to ask. It is also assumed is that the people will give the right answers. Both the assumptions are not always correct. Malinowski found that while the natives, the Trobriand Islanders, described a particular ceremony was solemn and serious in the questionnaire, in reality they were having fun during the ceremony. He understood that their responses did not correspond to the reality.

Suppose an anthropologist wants to study a tribe of cannibals. What kind of questions can he ask them? The questions would tend to represent his prejudices, something that is called **researcher imposition**. The questions could be based on ethno-centrism, looking at others' cultures with one's own culture as a reference. The more the gap between one's culture and that of the others one wants to study, the more there is scope for a questionnaire to become invalid.

When the researcher already knows many things about what he is studying and needs more data, then a questionnaire becomes valid. When there is a large gap between a researcher and the subject of his interest – a great distance between one's own culture and the culture being studied – then there is more likelihood for the questionnaire to become less valid. When anthropologists realised that getting to study a culture only through a questionnaire is completely wrong, the tradition of intensive field work began. An anthropologist undertakes intensive field work as an integral part of his career. He does graduation, goes on a field work for some years, then comes back and reports the field work, and only then will he be considered an anthropologist.

Some anthropologists go to study a second society so that their theory will not be conditioned by the study of only one society. Field work is more important in anthropology than in sociology because more distant cultures are studied in anthropology.

There is field work and participant-observation in sociology also. A transgender European sociologist was studying transgender people in India. She was shocked by the kind of discrimination transgenders in India were facing, and how they were being used as sex workers, forced to do many humiliating sexual acts. How did the researcher go about her study? She went to the transgender communities and interviewed them in groups. This is a technique called **focussed groups**. The fact that she is also a transgender endeared her to the transgender communities. They responded well. She moved from one group to another. During her extensive interactions, she interviewed many people, and she stayed for a reasonable amount of time with them. That is how field work is carried out. Note that this approach involves observation but not participant-observation. In participant-observation, one actually participates in the activities of the group of study. In a study of betting, a researcher may participate in betting to understand it better. That is participant-observation. But he would not be able to participate in some criminal activity when he is studying it. Still, he can move around with the criminals and do the field work for days. Prostitution also can be studied similarly. Staying around will give insights which cannot be obtained through mere questionnaires.

Observation is different from a questionnaire and an interview. In a questionnaire, you are depending on the respondent's response, but in observation, you are directly observing for yourself. Observation can be done either from outside or through participation. The method that one should develop depends also on what one wants to study and how much one knows already. For example, to understand criminal behaviour, can a questionnaire work? Obviously, no. The respondents can't be expected to give honest answers. So it can be studied only thorough observation that is combined with interviews. A sociologist can study the life in a slum through participant-observation. One can live in a slum, face the day-to-day problems, and then see how it goes.

Village communities can of course be studied through participant observation. M.N. Srinivas and Andre Beteille did so. Both of them are considered anthropologists as well as sociologists.

4.Life-history

One can also study a person as a case study. What does the movie Godfather show? It shows the story of one family, how one person rose from humble beginnings and started a mafia gang. Through that person you get to know how the mafia and the entire underground subculture operates. What does the movie Satya show? Its director Ram Gopal Varma was influenced by the characters of Godfather. Satya focusses on the life of the protagonist, it shows how one simple person coming from nowhere became an underground gang leader. This is the life-history method.

What method could Ram Gopal Varma have used to get the material for his movie? Did he conduct surveys? No. How did he make anohter movie Rakta Charitra? It is a movie based on real events and real people. How might he have made that movie, using what method? How did he study his subject? Ram Gopal Varma used the method of interview. To ask the right questions in an interview, he should know a lot about what was happening. Where would he get that information? Did he go to do field work? Was he doing observation? Was he there at the site of a murder? We can't say it was observation. He simply used the newspapers and the media. He read about these people. He got some clues and links, and then he went about interviewing the people.

There is a problem with the interview method. Will everybody readily agree to give an interview? Not likely. In fact, regarding his more recent movie 'Lakshmi's NTR', Ram Gopal Varma said, "Those who witnessed the scene are not going to tell me anything. I don't know them, they will not tell me anything, and even if they tell me something, I don't think they will tell the truth. We don't really have an account of what happened to N T Rama Rao in those days. So, I talked to people whether they were around at that time or not, and then I worked out what could be a plausible truth, because we don't know the actual truth." This is what he said regarding the method he followed. How far it was successful is a different thing. Despite the great effort that might have went into its research, I think the movie failed to bring out the complexities of the situation.

A study like what Ram Gopal Varma did to make Rakta Charitra is impossible to do through questionnaires. First, there were the interviews, then the cross-checking, then going through the life histories, then understanding how factionalism works, how crime works, and how politics operates. These are the various aspects of the groundwork he had to do to make the movie.

This is not to suggest that a life-history as a part of research is similar to making a biopic. A movie can create events and characters that bring out a theme, a researcher of course cannot do that.

5.More methods

Content analysis is the study of recorded human communications. Among the forms suitable for study are books, magazines, web pages, poems, newspapers, songs, speeches, and social media. Content analysis involves studying attitudes at any given time as well as the process of social change. It can also be used to compare different societies.

Content analysis will help when we want to know, for example, whether the incidents of factionalism are down or up Nowadays factionalism is down when compared to the past. Similarly, we can know whether Naxalism is down or up. What is content analysis? See the headlines related to your topic, see from where the reports are being made, read what views are being expressed in it by various sections of the people. You can know how the society is responding to the incidents reported. How did the society respond to a recent rape? How did it respond a few years ago? How did the society respond when the rape victim was a Dalit girl in a village? These kinds of questions are studied by content analysis.

One can study social change by content analysis. What do TV serials represent? Why some bad movies are successful while some good movies are not? What are people liking and not liking? Why something like Article 370 was not an issue, and why did so many people agitate about the Citizenship Amendment Bill? What does this show about Indians' attitude towards Kashmir? It is through exploring such questions that you can get to know people's perceptions.

A distinction is made between a primary source and a secondary source. A **secondary source** means any information that you are not generating. When you are generating information through questionnaires, then that is a **primary source**. When you are doing the interview, that becomes a primary source, but if you are going by interview done by somebody else, or by somebody's article or book, you are following secondary sources. The word 'secondary sources' does not mean that they are inferior in any way, it simply means you have not created them.

Oral historymeans some historical event narrated through oral means. To know about the Army action in Hyderabad at the time of its liberation in the 50s, you can still ask some people their experiences of it. That would constitute oral history. A lot of data regarding the Freedom Movement was generated through the method of oral history. When Gandhiji came to Tenali in Andhra Pradesh, for example, who were the people who gathered at the meeting, what did Gandhi talk, whom did he bless, how did people feel like? All that data comes under oral history. Is it a primary source or a secondary source? If it is being done by you, it is a primary source, if it is a collection of recorded interviews of others, then it is a secondary source. Oral history will be the only kind of history available if there is no written record at all. In a non-literate society that hasn't been studied yet, the history of its people can be known only through interviewing living people.

Genealogymeans all marriage and kinship links, how one person is connected to another. Father, mother, father's brothers, mother's sisters, mother's brothers, their father, grandfather, connections, all the consanguineal and affinal links. Consanguineal means related by blood, affinal means related by marriage. How is genealogy important? Through this method, one can understand types of kin groups– bilateral, matrilineal, patrilineal – and their role.

A considerable part of a society can be understood through marriage links. A genealogy can show things like caste endogamy, clan exogamy, patri-cross, matri-cross types of marriage and their implications.

6. *Sampling*

Populationin a survey research refers to the total group under study. **Sample** refers to a part of the population one wants to study. A sample should be adequate and representative of the population. Sampling refers to how we take a sample from the population.

Suppose the elections are coming and you want to find out whether the Chief Minister of Andhra Pradesh, Jagan Mohan Reddy, is likely to win again. How will you do it? Usually a questionnaire is used. You will conduct an opinion poll. Who will determine the outcome of the election? It is the voters of AP. The voters constitute the population in the survey. Population doesn't mean all the people in a region, but just those people whose behaviour we are going to study, here it means all the people eligible to vote. But can we administer a questionnaire to every single voter? It is not possible. It can be done only to a sample.

Only when this sample is representative would our study be valid. What is meant by validity of an opinion poll? It should be able to predict correctly which party is going to win. The opinion poll also has to be reliable. Reliability refers to the condition of the same results coming if the same methods are used on the same population. When the method and the population are fixed, then the outcome should be the same. Reliability is nothing but repeatability, independent of the researcher, but not independent of the method.

How will you select a sample such that their preferences best reflect the preferences of the population? Only when this happens can we say there is no sampling error. **Sampling error**refers to the errors committed in selecting the sample. The sample is selected from a sampling frame. **Sampling frame**refers to an accurate list of the units of the total population under study. AP electoral list of all the voters is the sampling frame in this case.

But will you go to the three districts in the northern Andhra Pradesh and conduct an opinion poll there and then say it is true for the whole of AP? Should you not visit all the regions instead? What are the three broad geographical divisions in AP? Rayalaseema, Coastal Andhra, and the northern districts. The sample should proportionately represent the people from all these three regions. If more voters are coming from Rayalaseema, then the sample should have more people from there. So you have to first identify a variable, and in this case the region is a variable. And then you identify how many people there are from that region. Can you name another variable? It would be caste. How do Reddys think? How do Kammas think? And how do the other castes behave? In a sample, you should pay attention to the caste factor. And then how about gender? Would man-woman differences figure in?

Sometimes we may not be able to identify what variables are important. If you think gender would play a role, then that the sample should reflect the sex ratio of the population. If you don't think gender would play a role, then you can ignore it. That's the problem in sampling, we need to know what the variables are to get the right sample.

Class is another variable – the rich, the middle class, and the poor. But how do you operationalise a class? We can't ask the people to which class they belong, the occupation and incomes can be known though. We also have to consider the beneficiaries of the welfare programs. Because of these various factors, it is not easy to get a right sample. Sampling requires a thorough knowledge of the variables, what factors are likely to influence the outcome, and the identified variables should be proportionately represented.

Consider a sample of three variables of gender, caste and region. If one Reddy woman from Rayalaseema is not responding, then the researcher will go for another Reddy woman from Rayalaseema. As long as the variables are matched, the individuals are not important. That's what **quota sampling**is. In quota sampling, people are not identified. And in case the survey gets responses from more people than required, the extra numbers will be discarded. If more Reddy women responded than needed, some of the responses will be discarded. Quota sampling in an opinion poll addresses the issue of representativeness, it involves identifying the number of people with a particular set of characteristics and taking their opinions.

In quota sampling, an unwilling person is replaced with a willing one, which in itself may constitute bias. People who are willing may have a particular preference, in which case this willingness itself may bring in a bias. An alternative to quota sampling is when they have these variables based on which they identify the people, and only those people have to answer, not their replacements. This is called stratified systematic sampling. This is based on probability sampling. Quota sampling is not probability sampling.

Random samplingor **simple random sampling**refers to selecting a sample in which each unit of the population has an equal chance of being included in the sample. If you want a sample of 10 out of population of 100, give numbers to all, select 10 numbers randomly and take the people corresponding to those numbers. On the other hand, from the same list, if you take every 10[th]person, with a random start, then it will be called **systematic sampling.** This is as good as or better than random sampling, but if the list has a particular order, then systematic sampling can contain errors. For example, if you take every 8[th]house in an apartment, the sample may contain particular type of houses, given the design of the apartment.

Stratified samplingrefers to dividing the population into strata and taking random samples from each one of the strata depending on the size of the stratum. Sampling error is caused by two reasons – sample size too small, or population is not homogeneous. Dividing the population into stages reduces the error caused by heterogeneity. For example, assign numbers to men first, then to women and pick up every 10[th]with random start. This way when you select 10, there will be 5 men and 5 women – making the sample representative of the population on the basis of gender.

Stratified systematic sampling involves listing all the people in the population. But if the population is too huge, listing all of them is not possible. Here comes **multistage sampling**. Instead of listing people, you can list blocks and get a sample of blocks. That is the first stage. Then you get a sample of households. And then a sample of people. This is sampling done in stages. The principles of stratified sampling can be applied at any stage of sampling to reduce sampling error.

Sometimes non-representative sampling is also used. **Non-representative sampling**may be used to disprove something. For example, a constituency has been voting consistently for a particular party. If you learn that even that constituency is not going to vote for this party this time, then it is less likely for that party to win. Non-representative sampling also happens in interviewing people to know their opinions. Usually only well-informed people can be called for an interview when studying something, but they are unrepresentative. However, only through them can you get to know more. It is not important that your cases should always be representative. If you know how they are unrepresentative, then they will serve a different purpose. This is also called **purposive sampling**, sampling done with a purpose.

Next there is **voluntary sampling**. It means inviting people to volunteer, and it could be biased. This is also an example of non-probability sampling. **Snowball sampling** is another non-probability sampling that refers to the process of accumulation as each located subject suggests other subjects. It means moving from one contact to another contact. A researcher studying criminality will get to know one criminal, and maybe from him he will go to another criminal. All of them cannot be assembled at one place and given questionnaires.

Key Terms

1. **Theoretical orientation**is a general attitude about how phenomena are to be explained.

2. **Theory**is an explanation of associations.

3. **Statistical association**or a **law**refers to correlation between two or more variables that is unlikely to be due to chance.

4. **Variable**is a thing or quantity that varies.

5. **Explanation**is an answer to a why question.

6. Quantitative analysisis analysis based on precise measurement.

7. Qualitative analysis deals with information that is not quantified.

8. Surveyis a systematic gathering of information about a large number of individuals and their communities using oral and written questioning, administering tools such as questionnaire and interview schedules and then interpreting the data by applying statistical methods.

9. Questionnaireis a survey tool consisting of a set of questions which is self-administered by the respondent.

10. Interviewis a method of data collection where information is gathered through oral questioning.

11. Interview schedule in terms of its structure is a schedule identical to a questionnaire, but in this, the interviewer asks the questions and notes down the respondent's answers verbatim.

12. Closed-ended questions, also known as 'forced-choice', 'fixed-response' and 'fixed-choice' questions, limit (or force) the respondent to choose responses from the categories already provided.

13. Open-ended questions, also termed 'free-response questions', do not have response options, instead give sufficient space to write (or dictate) his/her answer to the question.

14. Respondentis the person who answers questions in an interview session or in a survey.

15. Operational definitionmeans measurement of concept, which implies the empirical measurement of a verbal concept.

16. Reliability indicates the extent to which repeated measurements under the same conditions produce the same, consistent results.

17. Validityindicates where the findings are in agreement with theoretical or conceptual values.

18. Case studyis an in-depth and comprehensive study of a social unit – be that unit a person, a group, a social institution, a district, a community or a society. This is a part of qualitative approach.

19. Participant observationrefers to living among the people being studied – observing, questioning and (when possible) taking part in the important events of the group; writing or otherwise recording notes on observations, questions asked and answered, and things to check out later are parts of participant – observation.

20. Field work refers to first hand experience with the people being studied and the usual means by which anthropological information is being obtained.

21. Content analysis is the study of recorded human communications. Among the forms suitable for study are books, magazines, web pages, poems, newspapers, songs, speeches and social media.

22. Populationin a survey research refers to the total group under study.

23. Sample refers to a part of the population one wants to study. A sample should be adequate and representative of the population.

24. Sampling errorrefers to the errors committed in selecting the sample. The sample is selected from sampling frame.

25. Sampling framerefers to an accurate list of the units of the total population under study.

Think on it

1. How is methodology different from method? Give an example.

2. How is technique different from method? Give examples.

3. How is a theoretical orientation different from theory?

4. How is a theory different from a law or a statistical association?

5. How is a positivist different from a non-positivist?

6. What is a questionnaire?

7. What is an interview?

8. How is the quantitative approach different from the qualitative approach?

9. How is an open-ended question different from a closed-ended question?

10. How is interview schedule different from a questionnaire?

11. What is a survey?

12. What is an operational definition?

13. What is the difference between reliability and validity?

14. Who is a respondent?

15. What is a case study approach?

16. What are the advantages of a case study approach?

17. What is participant-observation? How is it different from observation?

18. What is field work? Why is it important in anthropology?

19. How useful is a method of life history to understand society?

20. What is content analysis?

21. What is the difference between a primary source and a secondary source?

22. What is oral history?

23. What is the role of genealogy in anthropological research?

24. How is a sample different from population?

25. What is a sampling error?

26. What is a sampling frame?

27. What is quota sampling?

28. How is random sampling different from systematic sampling?

29. What is the advantage of stratified sampling?

30. How is multi-stage sampling different from stratified sampling? Can both go together?

31. What is non-representative sampling?

32. What is voluntary sampling?

33. What is snowball sampling?

CHAPTER FIVE

Types of Economy

For over two million years, humans and hominins obtained their food by gathering wild plants, hunting wild animals, scavenging, and fishing. Agriculture was mostly unknown till 12,000 years ago. Most economies before the advent of the agriculture were **subsistence economies**in which almost all able-bodied men were largely engaged in getting food for themselves and their families.

1. Foraging

Foraging may be defined as a strategy to get food from wild plants and animal resources through gathering, hunting, scavenging or fishing. This is also known as **food collection**. Foragers are commonly called **hunter-gatherers**. Hunter-gatherers collect food from naturally occurring resources, that is, wild plants, animals and fish.

Foragers have some common characteristics. Most of them live in small communities in sparsely populated territories and follow a nomadic life. They do not recognise an individual's land rights. They have no classes. They have no full-time political heads. Division of labour is mostly based on age and gender.

Studies of two Australian aboriginial groups and another study of the !Kung group in Africa indicate that these foragers do not spend many hours getting food (McCarthy and McArthur, 1960) (R. B. Lee 1979). The !Kung adults spend on average of about 17 hours per week collecting food. After adding to it the time spent on toolmaking (6 hours per week) and housework (19 hours per week), it is clear that the !Kung people have more leisure time than many farmers.

Foraging societies that depend heavily on fishing (such as those in the Pacific Northwest or on the south coast of New Guinea) are more likely to have bigger and more permanent communities and more social inequality than foraging societies elsewhere that depend mostly on game and plants.

2. Horticulture

Horticulturerefers to plant cultivation carried out with relatively simple tools and methods. Nature is allowed to replace nutrients in the soil in the absence of permanently cultivated fields. The tools employed are usually hand tools such as the digging stick or hoe, not ploughs and other equipment. And the methods used in horticulture do not include fertilization, irrigation, or other ways to restore soil fertility after a growing season.

There are two types of horticulture. **Extensive cultivation**is a type of horticulture in which the land is worked for short periods and then left to regenerate for some years before being used again. This is also called **shifting cultivation**. During the years when the land is not cultivated, wild plants and brush grow on it. **Slash-and-burn**is a form of extensive cultivation in which the natural vegetation is cut down and burned off. The cleared ground is used for a short period and then left to regenerate. **Swidden agriculture** is a scholarly term for extensive cultivation or slash-and-burn. The other kind of horticulture involves a dependence on long-growing tree crops. The two kinds of horticulture may be practised by the same society, but in neither case there is a permanent cultivation of field crops.

Most horticultural societies do not rely on crops alone for food, they also hunt and fish. A few are nomadic for some months in an year. Often horticulturalists raise small animals such as pigs, chicken, goats, and sheep.

As opposed to extensive cultivation,**intensive agriculture**is food production characterised by the permanent cultivation of fields and made possible by the use of the plough, draft animals or machines, fertilisers, irrigation, water-storage techniques, and other complex agricultural techniques. The agriculture that is done in Indian villages is intensive agriculture.

3. Pastoralism

Pastoralism is a form of subsistence technology in which food-getting is based directly or indirectly on the maintenance of domesticated animals.

Pastoralists often get their protein intake from live animals in the form of milk, and some regularly use their blood, which is rich in proteins, mixing it with other foods. Many pastoralists trade animal products for plant foods and other necessities. A large proportion of their food may actually come from trade with agricultural groups living around them.

The Toda who inhabit the Nilgiri Hills are pastoralists whose economy revolves around buffaloes. Some of these buffaloes are regarded as sacred, they are kept separately and their dairy preparations are accompanied with rituals. Women's position is inferior to men in the Toda society. All the dairy-related activities including cooking are performed only by men. The society is divided into endogamous moieties. A moiety is one of the two basic subdivisions of a trbie. These moieties are hierarchically positioned – as all the sacred dairies are owned by one moiety. A moiety has exogamous clans. The Toda practise fraternal polyandry.

The Toda have other tribes as close neighbours – the Badaga, the Kota and the Kurumba. The Toda share equal status with the Badaga, the Kota and the Kurumba have a lower status. The Kota are blacksmiths and musicians, they also make utensils. The Badaga are farmers. The Kurumba serve the Badaga as agricultural labourers. The Toda trade their products with the goods and services produced by their neighbours.

Terms

1. Subsistence economiesare economies in which almost all able-bodied men are largely engaged in getting food for themselves and their families.

2. Foraging / food collection refers to a strategy to get food from wild plant and animal resources through gathering, hunting, scavenging or fishing.

3. Hunter-gatherersare the people who collect food from naturally occurring resources, that is, wild plants, animals and fish.

4. Pastoralism is a form of animal husbandry in which food-getting is based directly or indirectly on the maintenance of domesticated animals.

5. Horticulturerefers to plant cultivation carried out with relatively simple tools and methods; nature is allowed to replace nutrients in the soil, in the absence of permanently cultivated fields.

6. Extensive (shifting) cultivationis a type of horticulture in which the land is worked for short periods and then left to regenerate for some years before being used again.

7. Slash-and-burnis a form of extensive cultivation in which the natural vegetation is cut down and burned off. The cleared ground is used for a short period and then left to regenerate.

8. Swidden agriculture is the scholarly term for extensive cultivation or slash-and-burn.

9. Intensive agricultureis food production characterised by the permanent cultivation of fields and made possible by the use of the plow, draft animals or machines, fertilisers, irrigation, water-storage techniques, and other complex agricultural techniques.

Think on it

1. What is meant by a subsistence economy?
   2. What is foraging?
   3. Do foragers have more leisure than farmers?

4. Can foragers have social hierarchies? Explain.

5. Is slash-and-burn a form of extensive cultivation?

6. Is slash-and-burn a type of horticulture? What is the other type?

7. What is meant by Swidden agriculture?

8. What is intensive agriculture?

9. What is pastoralism?

10. With whom do the Toda trade? And in what goods?

CHAPTER SIX

Modes of Exchange

We are going to discuss modes of exchange, that is, exchange of goods and services, in simple societies. We will see the differences in economic transactions between simple societies and complex societies. The political economist Karl Polanyi identified three systems of exchange. He said the modes of exchange follow different patterns in simple systems as compared to complex systems.

1. Market, reciprocity, redistribution

Let's consider complex systems first. Our present-day society is a complex system. The basic exchange system that we follow is the market. Most of the goods and services in our society are interchanged through the market mechanism. A market is something that goes by demand and supply mechanism. People want to buy at a lower price, they will buy something more when its price is less. People want to sell something at a higher price, they want to sell it more when its price is high. In this system, both the buyer and the seller want to maximise their gains.

And then people have different choices to make. A buyer can buy from Company A or Company B. He can buy different products; he can buy tea or he can buy coffee. There are a variety of products and sellers in the market, and a buyer has to choose between them. He will make his choices on the basis of reason. This approach is called rational choice. It is driven by considerations of low price and high quality for any particular product. Among all the products available, a buyer picks only certain products in accordance with his needs and tastes. When the needs and tastes are fulfilled, he derives satisfaction. A buyer wants to maximise his satisfaction with minimum resources. He calculates, he reasons and decides.

A buyer is therefore a selfish, calculating, and rational person. He will buy from whoever is selling at a lower price within a satisfactory range of quality. The market does not assume a relationship between the buyer and the seller – no relationship that will last, no obligations. A market system is based on transactions of purely economic nature. If one is buying something from the other, it is not out of friendship or any such personal considerations, it is simply because of lower price, compared to the price of its alternative. This is what is called economic behaviour in the context of a market. In complex societies, most of the exchange is taking place through the market mechanism.

Note that the market exchange does not necessarily denote a physical place. **Market exchange**, also called **commercial exchange**,refers to transactions in which the prices are subject to demand and supply, whether or not the transactions occur in a market place.

The market exchange is not the only kind of economic transaction in a complex society. How can the give-and-take transactions within a family be characterised? Within a family, the parents give a lot to the children. This is also a kind of exchange. This is called generalised reciprocity.

Reciprocityrefers to giving and taking without the use of money. There are two kinds of reciprocity, generalised and balanced. **Generalised reciprocity**refers to gift giving without any immediate or planned return. **Balanced reciprocity**refers to giving with the expectation of a straightforward immediate or limited-time trade.

Between parents and children, the parents keep giving even if the children may probably never reciprocate in any way in the future. Generalised reciprocity is a kind of gift, whereas in balanced reciprocity one person gives to another person expecting more or less something of equal value in return. It is a balanced transaction.

In Indian villages, transactions happened mostly through reciprocity down the ages. Castes were linked to each other through it. Only recently money became a part of the economic transactions in these villages. In the olden days, there was more balanced reciprocity; in the modern society, the role of balanced reciprocity dwindled as the market system became predominant.

There is one more mode of exchange, it is called redistribution. **Redistribution**refers to the accumulation of goods (or labour) by a particular person or in a particular place and their subsequent distribution.

People paying taxes to the government and the government spending that money on the people is an example of redistribution. The entire government in our democracy functions through redistribution. We have the market exchange, we have reciprocity and we have redistribution, but the market exchange is the most dominant mode.

2. Reciprocity among foragers

Reciprocity, and not the market exchange, is the most important mode of exchange in simple societies. Many studies illustrate this mode of exchange. Lorna Marshall (1961) recounted how the !Kung divided an eland, a large African antelope, brought to a site where five bands and several visitors were camping – more than 100 in all. The owner of the arrow that had first penetrated the eland was, by custom, the owner of the meat. He first distributed the forequarter to the two hunters who had aided him in the kill. After that, the distribution depended on kinship: each hunter shared the meat with his wife's parents, then with his wife, children, parents, and siblings, and they in turn shared some of the meat with their kin. This kind of distribution of large game – clearly a form of generalised reciprocity – is common among foragers.

Generalised reciprocity means 'I am giving, even if you don't give anything in return, now or later'. Why do people do this in the simple societies? Because the outcome of hunting is unpredictable. Today one person gets an animal but tomorrow he might not and another person might. Only through sharing meat freely among themselves, the people have better chances of survival on the whole. What is emphasised here? Sharing and giving. Sharing brings more certainty to a day's food for everyone.

The !Kung example of reciprocity reveals one more aspect of economy in simple societies. The reciprocity is taking place along kinship lines. Sharing is done as an obligation towards one's kin. The economic transaction is taking place in a social context.

When Lorna Marshall left the band in 1951, she gave each woman in the band a present of enough cowrie shells to make a necklace – one large shell and 20 small ones. When she returned in 1952, she found no cowrie shell necklaces and hardly a single shell among the people of the band. Instead, the shells appeared by ones and twos in the ornaments of the people of the neighbouring bands. Why did not the women keep the shells with themselves? If a woman kept the shells for herself, her behaviour would have been disapproved of. Having any possession is discouraged, sharing is encouraged.

Sharing is what is expected. It is not regarded as a gesture of generosity which has to be thanked for. When someone boasts of his kill, making others feel he has done them a favour, his behaviour is discouraged. Richard Lee (1969) recounts how he learned about it. To please the !Kung people with whom he was staying, he bought the largest and fattest ox in the region, to have it slaughtered as a present. One !Kung elder after another looked at it and said dismissive things about it, "Of course, we will eat it. But it won't fill us up. You are duped into buying a worthless animal." Lee was puzzled by their behaviour. He later got to know that the !Kung discourage anyone thinking highly of himself for giving too much to others.

While generalised reciprocity takes place within a society, balanced reciprocity takes place with regard to other societies. Vedda of Sri Lanka leave honey at a place expecting iron tools from the Sinhalese. If the Vedda think iron tools left by the Sinhalese are fair exchange, they will leave honey and take the tools, otherwise they will take back their honey!

3. Potlach

Now let's move beyond bands to societies where there is increased productivity, higher population density and the possibility of surplus. Under conditions of surplus, chiefdom evolves. A horticultural society may have a chief, even fishing communities may have chiefs when there is an abundance of food. The chiefs amass the resources of the society, only to give them away later. A chief does it because giving enhances his prestige. Prestige is a very important thing for a chief. Chiefs will compete with each other to have greater prestige.

In chiefdoms, redistribution is an important mode of exchange. The Kwakiutl in the Pacific Northwest have a tradition of holding a grand ceremony called a potlatch. The various chiefs of a region would organise an event, calling a large number people from villages all around.

A difference between a band society and a chiefdom is that in a band society, people are not supposed to hoard, they share whatever they have; whereas in a chiefdom, the chiefs first accumulate the resources and then give them away.

In a band society all the people are equal, there are no power differences or wealth differences among them. In a chiefdom, prestige differences arise. A chief and his family have a higher prestige than the others in the society. Hoarding is not a source of prestige, giving is. In a band society, boasting is disapproved of, but in a chiefdom, the chief keeps boasting. Ruth Benedict (1960) mentions a potlach speech, "I am the great chief who makes people ashamed. Our chief brings jealousy to the faces. I am the only great tree, I the chief."

Marvin Harris explains these boastful potlaches in terms of resource sharing. The chiefs should first be successful in organising labour to accumulate the resources necessary for giving feasts. Successful chiefs attract people from other villages to their own. The occasion of boasting is a reward for the acquisition of resources. The potlatch is also a part of a sharing system. Those who have are giving to those who do not have. This is also a way of managing shortages. The group that is taking now may be giving later. Though there is an overall abundance in the regions of the northwestern coast of North America, they experience alternating periods of plenty and shortage.

Now, what's the difference between a chiefdom and a kingdom? In a chiefdom, whatever is accumulated will mostly go back to the people. The chief will not hoard. By the time the chiefdom evolves into a kingdom however, the king takes a lot from his subjects and gives relatively less back to them. The king has wealth, power, and prestige. He also has a powerful army to enforce his will.

4. Market in simple societies

As simple societies evolve into more complex societies, the market system also evolves.

In a simple society, a market is held at a specific place for a specific time and for a limited range of goods. People will assemble for the exchange. There may be some kind of money involved. That money may be **special purpose money**– which refers to objects of value for which only some goods and services can be exchanged. Shells could be used as currency, but they may buy only a particular range of products and not anything.

This money is not like the money in our society which can be used to buy many goods and services. Ours is **general purpose money**, which is a universally accepted medium of exchange. Trade based on the market exchange and the availability of general purpose money is associated with the evolution of the state.

5. Economic Anthropology

Economic anthropology focusses on two aspects of economics: 1) provisioning, which is the collection, production and distribution of goods and services, and 2) the strategy of economising, often put in terms of the substantivist-formalistdebate. This debate is covered in detail in my *Anthropological Thought*.

It studies the level of technology, division of labour, the nature of skills used to collect or produce food under each type of economy. It studies how goods and services are distributed as economies evolve,. It studies how distribution systems move from egalitarian to stratified. It also studies social structure, how population is organised. It studies ownership patterns and how an economic organisation shapes and is shaped by its political organisation. It also studies what drives change – is it technology or population density or both? It also investigates the role of diffusion of cultural traits in altering technology, economy and society.

Terms

1. Market (commercial) exchange refers to transaction in which the prices are subject to supply and demand, whether or not the transactions occur in a market place.

2. Reciprocityrefers to giving and taking without the use of money.

3. Generalised reciprocityrefers to gift giving without any immediate or planned return.

4. Balanced reciprocityrefers to giving with the expectation of a straightforward immediate or limited-time trade.

5. Redistributionrefers to the accumulation of goods (or labour) by a particular person or in a particular place and their subsequent distribution.

6. Potlach refers to feast among Pacific Northwest Native Americans at which great quantities of food and goods are given to the guests in order to gain prestige for the host.

7. Special purpose moneyrefers to objects of value for which only some goods and services can be exchanged.

8. General purpose moneyis a universally accepted medium of exchange.

• 59 •

Think on it

1. What is meant by market exchange? Explain its chief features.

2. How is generalised reciprocity different from balanced reciprocity?

3. What is redistribution?

4. Which mode of exchange is more dominant in a complex society?

5. How does reciprocity work among foragers?

6. Is a forager less selfish? If so, why? Does it mean he is a better human being?

7. What political function does a potlatch serve?

8. How does potlatch involve redistribution as well as reciprocity?

9. Explain how economic transactions in simple societies are embedded in social and political contexts.

10. How is general purpose money different from special purpose money?

11. How is the market in simple societies different from the one in complex societies?

12. List the differences in the economies of complex societies and simple societies.

13. Explain the scope of economic anthropology.

CHAPTER SEVEN

Political Organisation

By political organisation, we mean how power and control-related structures function in a society. One way of studying it is to look at the political structure of our own society, and then go back to its primitive forms.

1. Nation and state

What is our political structure? Our nation is also a state. What is meant by nation and what is meant by state? According to Max Weber, the **state**is that «human community that (successfully) claims the monopoly of the legitimate use of violence within a given territory.» When something is a state, we mean that there is somebody – it can be a king with an army – who controls it. He has a monopoly over the coercive power exercise in it. Put in simpler terms, the presence of an effective army in a territory makes it a state.

Our state has also another characteristic. The people living within the bounds of this territory are not only controlled by the state power, but they also think that this land is theirs. That is, there is a sense of belongingness. This sense of belongingness among the people makes our state a nation.

The feeling we have that we are Indians is because we are a nation. Akbar's **kingdom** was not a nation. The Vijayanagara kingdom was not a nation. They were only states. But ours is a state as well as a nation. By state we mean effective control. By nation we mean a sense of belongingness. India is a **nation-state** – the co-occurrence of a political state and a nation.

This nation-state has a constitution, a legislature, an executive, a judiciary, and an army. In this huge territory, we have many societies. What we call India is a nation-state, it is not a single society, there are so many societies in India. What is a society? A society is a culture-sharing group. India is a nation-state with many societies and many cultures.

A nation refers to a feeling, a state refers to control. Ours is a nation-state. We are supposed to have the feeling of belongingness, and there is also supposed to be an effective state control over us. But it is not a uniform thing. There are many groups of people who don't think they should belong to this country, and there are some areas within India where the Army doesn't have control. So India is not thorougly a nation nor is it thoroughly a state. When we make nation-building an ideal, we mean that we are not a complete nation yet and we should become a better nation. The nation is about a sentiment. Promotion of this sentiment is nationalism. **Nationalism**refers to the strong sense of loyalty, attachment and devotion to one's nation.

2. Band organisation

What is the political structure in a hunting-gathering society? To know about it, you first need to be clear about certain terms.

First, what is a community? Community means a group of people who know one another. What is the difference between a society and a community? Communities put together form a society.

Societies at a hunting-gathering stage have small groups called bands. **Band** is a fairly small, usually nomadic local group that is politically autonomous. In a band, people know one another, so we say a band is a community.

Anthropologists divide political organisations based on the level the political integration that takes place . They classify political organisations according to the highest stage at which the political integration takes place.

In hunting-gathering societies, bands have leaders, but there is no leader over the various bands. The leader of a band is called headman. There is nothing like a leader over more than one band. The highest level of political integration in a hunting-gathering society is therefore a band. Band as a kind of political organisation – band organisation – means that the centralisation of leadership is at the community level. What is the community here? It's a band. **Band organisation** refers to the kind of political organisation where the local group or band is the largest territorial group in the society that acts as a unit.

A band has a headman. He has no special power. He does not have more resources than the others in the band. His leadership is informal and confined to taking some important decisions. **Headman** is a person who holds a powerless but symbolically unifying position in a community within an egalitarian society.

These are **egalitarian societies,** which means these are societies in which all the people of a given age-sex category have equal access to economic resources and prestige. Societies at the level of band organisation do not have classes. **Class societies** are societies containing social groups that have unequal access to economic resources, power and prestige.

3. Tribal organisation

We will now look at the next stage, the tribe. 'Tribe' is a little ambiguous word and many Indian students get confused about it. We are discussing tribe as a type of political organisation here. This is not a 'tribe' in the sense we use the word in India. Here 'tribe' does not refer to a group which is not a caste, tribe as a political organisation is a different concept.

Tribe refers to a territorial population in which there are kin or nonkin groups with representatives in a number of local groups. **Tribal organisation** refers to the kind of political organisation in which local communities mostly act autonomously but there are kin groups (such as clans) or associations (such as age-sets) that can temporarily integrate a number of local groups into a lager unit.

When political structures exist across communities, then anthropologists say that that society has a tribal organisation. When does tribal organisation happen? It happens often when there is extensive agriculture. Some good examples of such a tribal organisation are segmentary lineages and age-sets.

The Karimojong of Uganda have age sets. Their society is divided into four distinct generation-sets: the uninitiated boys, the juniors, the seniors and the retired. A generation set consists of a combination of five age sets, covering 25 to 30 years. The senior generation set exercises authority. They perform administrative, judicial and priestly functions. Members of the junior generation set serve as warriors and police. The retired generation set consists of the elders who passed on their authority. Age sets like these reinforce the society's preparedness to fight a war, by supplementing kin-based groups.

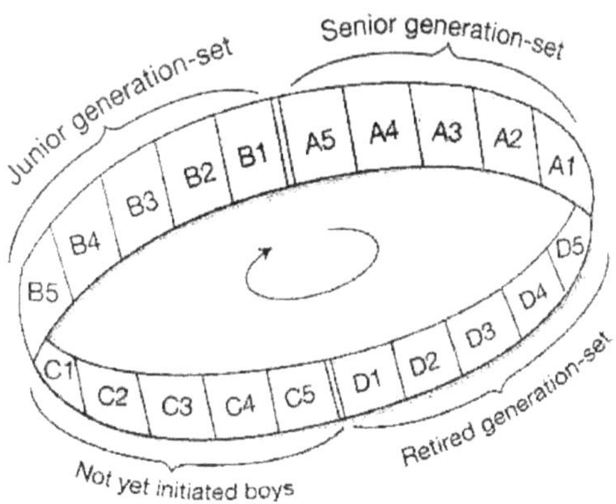

Fig 7.1: Age sets

The Tiv of Nigeria have segmentary lineage system. The society is composed of segments, every segment belongs to a hierarchy of lineages stretching farther and farther back genealogically. A segment unites against another segment in case of conflict. Their ideology is summed up like this: "I against my brothers; my brothers and I against our cousins; my brothers and cousins and I against the world."

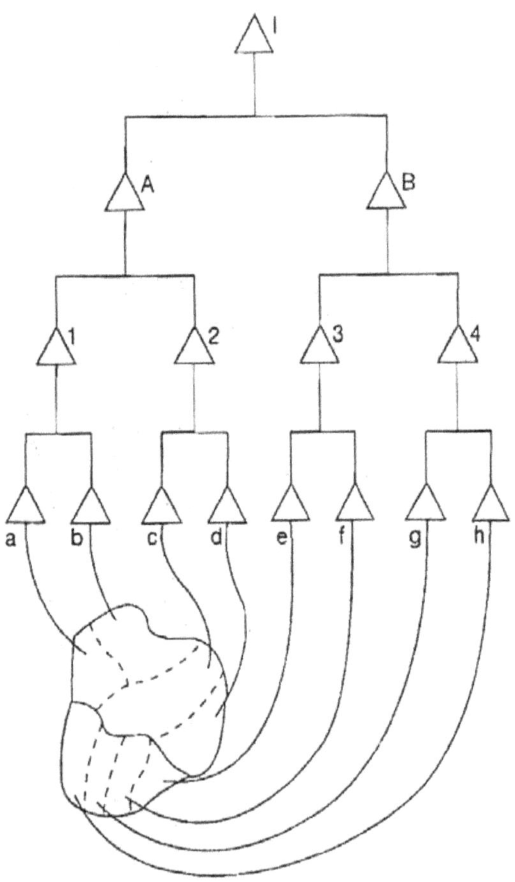

Fig. 7.2: Tiv lineage segments

When a person of lineage (a) quarrels with a member of lineage (b), the lineages of (a) and (b) will come into conflict. If the same person quarrels with a person of lineage (c), the segments (1) and (2) enter conflict. If the same person quarrels with a person of lineage (e), then segments (A) and (B) will come into conflict. Of course, more serious issues would be needed to involve more number of people.

The Nuer of the Greater Upper Nile region were in many ways similar to their neighbours, the Dinka – except that the Nuer had a segmentary lineage system. The Nuer could make incursions into the Dinka territory because of the military advantage that the segmentary lineage system conferred on them. Segmentary lineage system is a source of strength.

4. *Chiefdom*

In a chiefdom, you have a chief or a council. This chiefdom can be either for an entire society or for only a part of it. It is not necessary that the entire society should have a chief or a council.

Usually, chiefdom happens when there is extensive or intensive agriculture. A chiefdom is not a class-based society, but the chief and his family may have a higher prestige which is why we call a chiefdom a ranked society. The chief and his family would have higher prestige but not more power or economic resources than the other people in the society. The chiefs often accumulate goods but only to give them away. They don't develop a standing army. Chiefs do not have much power. They simply have more prestige and honour or respect.

You call a society a state when there is an army, a king, taxation, and all such things. When states form, many societies can come under a state. A society may have one state, or a state may have many societies. In the modern age, the entire world is divided into nation-states.

Societies that are chiefdoms or states are called **state societies**. Societies with band organisation or tribal organisation are called **stateless societies**. During the course of history, in the battle between the state and the stateless, the states have expanded and absorbed the stateless. Simple societies that were absorbed by the states are fighting for their rights now. The state societies became extremely powerful over the centuries and colonised the entire world.

5. Power and authority

Max Weber defined **domination** as "the probability that certain specific commands will be obeyed by a given group of persons." Weber was interested in finding out legitimate forms of domination. He called legitimate form of domination **authority**.

Weber classified authority into three kinds: legal-rational, traditional, and charismatic. The **legal-rational authority** rests "on a belief in the legality of enacted rules and the right of those elevated to authority under such rules to issue commands." A government officer's source of authority is legal-rational. Traditional authority refers to authority derived from tradition. A father may exercise his traditional authority over his family. The charismatic authority rests on the devotion of the followers to the exceptional qualities of a leader. Some politicians and religious gurus may have this kind of authority.

To Weber, authority has legitimacy but power does not. A minister forcing a collector to implement a scheme efficiently is an example of authority, but the same minister forcing a collector to give a contract to his nephew is an example of power. Both power and authority are ways of controlling the people – the difference lies only in the degree of **legitimacy**.

Terms

1. **State** is an autonomous political unit with centralized decision making over many communities with power to govern by force.

2. **Nation** refers to a set of people sharing a common territory, history and a sense of identity.

3. **Nation-state** refers to the co-occurrence of a political state and a nation.

4. **Nationalism** refers to the strong sense of loyalty, attachment and devotion to a nation.

5. **Band** is a fairly small, usually nomadic local group that is politically autonomous.

6. **Band organisation** refers to the kind of political organization where the local group or band is the largest territorial group in the society that acts as a unit.

7. **Headman** is a person who holds a powerless but symbolically unifying position in a community within an egalitarian society; may exercise influence but has no power to impose sanctions.

8. **Tribe** refers to a territorial population in which there are kin or nonkin groups with representatives in a number of local groups.

9. **Tribal organisation** refers to the kind of political organization in which local communities mostly act autonomously but there are kin groups (such as clans) or associations (such as age-sets) that can temporarily integrate a number of local groups into a lager unit.

10. **Segmentary lineage system** refers to a hierarchy of more inclusive lineages; usually functions only in a conflict situations.

11. **Complementary opposition** refers to the occasional uniting of various segments of a segmentary lineage system in opposition to similar arrangements.

12. **Age-set** refers to a group of people of similar age and the same sex who move together through some or all of life's stages.

13. **Age-grade** refers to a category of people who happen to fall within a particular, culturally distinguished age range.

14. **Chiefdom** is a political unit with a chief as its head, integrating more than one community but not necessarily the whole society or language group.

15. Chief is a person who exercises authority, usually on behalf of a multi-community political unit.

16. Rank societies are societies that do not have any unequal access to economic resources or power, but with social groups that have unequal access to status positions and prestige.

17. Prestige means being accorded particular respect or honour.

18. Power refers to the ability to make others do what they do not want to do or influence based on the threat of force.

19. Class societies are societies containing social groups that have unequal access to economic resources, power and prestige.

20. Egalitarian societies are societies in which all people of a given age-sex category have equal access to economic resources and prestige.

Think on it

1. What is Max Weber's definition of a state?
2. How is a state different from a nation?
3. Is kingdom a form of state?
4. What is a nation-state?
5. What is nationalism?
6. What is a band? Who is a headman?
7. What is a band organisation?
8. What is the difference between community and society?
9. At what level of economy, a society has band organisation?
10. How is an egalitarian society different from a class society?
11. What is a tribe? What is tribal organisation?
12. What do you know about age-sets?
13. Explain segmentary lineage system.
14. Can a society have more than one chief?
15. What is a rank society different from a class society?
16. Do all foragers have egalitarian societies?
17. What is the difference between power and authority?
18. How is power different from prestige?
19. Explain the concept of legitimacy according to Weber.

CHAPTER EIGHT

Law and justice in simple societies

Anthropologists seek to study law and social control. This is about how the individuals in a society are controlled by it. Let us first consider how individuals are controlled in a nation-state. You have a constitution, you have a legislature, you have a judiciary, you have an executive, you have the police, the jails – these are the ways our control systems work, ultimately backed by an army. And anthropologists want to find out what are the equivalent structures in simple societies.

Simple societies do not have a codified law. We have codified laws which are written. When a judge gives a punishment, he does it saying that a particular deed is unlawful and it requires a certain kind of punishment. The law is already existing, and the corresponding punishment for a violation of the law is also stipulated. These laws come from the legislature, and the legislature is created by the constitution.

Anthropologists wanted to know whether simple societies have laws at all. If they don't have a law, how is social order maintained? Here anthropology offers a very powerful insight. Anthropologist E. Adamson Hoebel says that in simple societies there is social control as well as law. Social control is not the same thing as law, it is more than law. There is law even in the simplest societies which are non-literate and which do not have any legislature. They have not written anything but, Hoebel says, they still have laws.

How is law different from social control? Hoebel says that a lot of social control is done through the socialisation process. People are asked to behave in a particular way through a system of reward and punishment, informally delivered. "Good boy," "good girl," "You can't do this, and if you do it, we wouldn't like you." The parents themselves punish the children. Hoebel says all these things are aspects of social control.

And what is a law? Hoebel says that law is something which comes into action where entities unconcerned with an offence enter the picture. A hit B, and in response, B hit A, there is no law there. People may think, yes, B has the right to hit A. When A hits B, B's parents hit A. There is no law there, it is accepted that you shouldn't hit others, and when others hit you, you shouldn't keep quiet. When does law come into existence? According to Hoebel, law comes in when those people who are not directly affected in the case enter the picture. In every society there is a way by which the society enters to punish a non-trivial violation of social code. Such an intervention by the society is what law is.

Hoebel defined law in this way: "Anthropologically considered, **law**is merely one aspect of our culture – the aspect that employs the force of organised society to regulate individual and group conduct and to prevent redress or punish deviations from prescribed social norms."

Now consider our institutions of law. Why are the judges punishing the accused? It's not because they are personally offended. Policemen, courts and jails – nothing is personal. Why are they doing what they are doing? Because the society has asked them to do it on its behalf. Even in the simplest of societies, there is an agreement that there are certain expected norms. And if those norms are violated beyond a point, then there are mechanisms by which the society intervenes to punish the violators. That is law. When anthropologists looked at how law is being implemented in primitive societies, they found that a variety of ways are employed.

Let us look at how law evolved. The difference between simple societies and complex societies, in terms of law, is that in simple societies, law is closer to the people. The people know what is right and what is wrong. Not only do they have consensus regarding what is right and what is wrong, but they are also more likely to know who the aggressor is. The complex societies are stratified, there are diverse groups and no common social code. In a nation-state, only because there is no common understanding among the people, you have a constitution. What does our constitution promise? Democracy, equality, protection of the rights of individuals and groups, and many such things.

To understand law in a simple society, consider an ordeal. An **ordeal** refers to a means of determining guilt or innocence by submitting the accused to dangerous or painful tests believed to be under supernatural control. Somebody puts his hand on something hot and then says, "If I am telling the truth, my hand shouldn't hurt." How does it work? Anthropologist Lawrence Rosen points out people simply know who is the wrong-doer. And then they punish him by forcing the ordeal

In complex societies there are power differences, some groups have more power, some regions have more power, some religions have more power. This kind of gap between various sections of the society is possible only with the modern states. Here, law can be very undemocratic and coercive. Capital punishment, delayed punishments, huge prison populations – this is the nature of the modern states.

Examples of law in simple societies

Franz Boas gives an example of law in Inuit societies. Padlu, a native of Padli, induced the wife of a native of another village to desert her husband and follow him. When the betrayed husband went to Padli to take revenge, he was killed. Then his brother was killed,, and then one of his relatives. Then the headman learnt of these developments, assessed the opinions of the natives of the village, took Padlu for deer hunting and killed him. The headman went by what the community wanted. This is an example of justice delivered through community action.

Amon the Nuer in Africa, leopard-skin chief is a mediator. His position is hereditary. If a person in the tribe kills somebody, he would go to this mediator whose house can be used as a sanctuary. Over some months, the chief mediates between the parties involved and arranges compensation for the victim's side, usually in the form of cattle. But he has no power to enforce a decision. This is an example of mediation.

Law among the Kamar is described by S.C. Dube. These people are at a food gathering stage even today. Many kinds of violations are believed to invite supernatural wrath – incest, for example. But legal action can also be taken. Incest leads to excommunication. A homicide can be pardoned if the criminal sponsors a feast for the villagers. Adultery, witchcraft, marrying a fifth one after changing four husbands are some of the acts considered as violations. Panchayats are involved in an adjudication where both sides are heard. The majority decides on the judgement. When the panchayat awards penal feast, as it does in many cases, it fixes the items for the feast according to the degree of violation. Some violations are met with fine. The elders are the guardians of law and order, they are its interpreters and adjudicators of disputes. There is no central authority for the entire tribe. A group of settlements have a panchayat. Elderly men constitute the panchayats. There is no authority above the panchayats. They rely upon eye witnesses too in a hearing. Personal disputes are sometimes settled through exchange of blows between the involved parties.

The Kharia are also at a food gathering stage. Penal feasts and excommunication are given as punishments by the panchayats.

The Rengma Naga had the institution of a chief who would be assisted by the leading men of different clans. If the chief is disobeyed by any member of the tribe, his house would be destroyed. Parties to a dispute do not plainly state their case before the chief. Instead, they cry hoarse and create confusion. Despite that, the old men have to arrive at the right decision. For serious offences like homicide or arson, the accused is exiled and his house is burnt. The exile is temporary though. For setting a fire to the jungle, collective cursing by the entire village is the punishment. For having sex with an unmarried girl, even if it is not against her will, a man might have to pay a fine to her parents, but that tainted money may be given to others or destroyed. Sometimes oaths are administered to find the truth and perjury is supposed to invite supernatural wrath.

Terms

1. Codified laws: formal principles for resolving disputes in heterogeneous and stratified societies.

2. Negotiation: the process by which the parties to a dispute try to resolve it themselves.

3. Mediation: the process by which a third-party tries to bring about a settlement in the absence of formal authority to force a settlement.

4. Oath: the act of calling upon a deity to bear witness to the truth of what one says.

5. Ordeal: a means of determining guilt or innocence by submitting the accused to dangerous or painful tests believed to be under supernatural control.

6. Adjudication: the process by which a third party acting as a judge makes a decision that the parties to a dispute have to accept.

Think on it

1. What are codified laws? Who have them?

2. What is the difference between social control and law?

3. What is justice?

4. Give Hoebel's definition of law.

5. How is mediation different from negotiation?

6. How is adjudication different from mediation?

7. How is an ordeal different from an oath?

8. Discuss the salient features of law in simple societies and contrast it with the law in complex societies.

Sex and Gender

We will explore the issue of gender differences, we will discuss why girls behave the way they do, and boys behave like boys. You know that girls and boys are expected to behave in certain ways, but the question is why girls and boys behave differently and what purpose does it serve. Do they behave differently simply because of socialisation or are there inherent biological differences? That is the core issue.

1. Sex and gender differences

Social anthropologists use two words: sexual differences and gender differences. **Sexual differences** refer to the typical the differences between females and males that are most likely due to biological differences. **Gender differences** refer to the differences between females and males that reflect cultural expectations and experiences.

By sexual and gender differences we mean differences in general – or on average. We do not mean any boy is different from any girl in this way. We mean boys in general are different from girls in general.. We see that, in general, boys are more aggressive. We are not saying that any particular boy is more aggressive than any particular girl. Typically, boys are more aggressive. Most people would accept that statement. But if you are asked if it is a result of socialisation or if it is biologically inherited, what would your answer be?

Are there any fundamental psychological differences between boys and girls and if so, are they inherited? There could be three possible answers here – a) entirely biological b) entirely a result of socialisation c) both biological and socialisation factors are involved. And even if we agree about both biological and social factors, we could still ask which of them may be more important.

Now, obviously there are socialisation differences. Boys are encouraged to be aggressive, they may be given guns as toys. Girls play with dolls and such..

When boys fight, the parents may encourage it. When a girl goes and hits somebody, parents will discourage it. So there are socialisation differences, but are there inherent biological differences as well that explain different behaviours? Even if there are, how could we find out?

2. Sexual dimorphism

Sexual dimorphism refers to a marked difference in size and appearance between males and females of a species. Let us work out what the main physical differences are, other than sexual organs.

Take the aspect of height. Girls are generally shorter. Till a particular age, boys and girls grow at the same pace. In fact, at some stage in the high school, girls may be bigger than boys. After puberty, girls grow for some time and stop, but boys continue to grow for a longer time and become taller.

But why should this be so in nature? Why should boys be taller on average? The evolutionary explanation is that a larger portion of the nutrition a young woman takes goes into developing her reproductive mechanism, and there is an early cessation of her growth in height. If she continues to use it for her own growth then the child will suffer. She reaches a particular height and stays there. In this way, the physiological difference in height is explained through natural selection.

Natural selection refers to the outcome of the processes that affect the frequencies of traits in a particular environment. The traits that enhance survival and reproductive success increase in frequency over time. Giraffe is a good example to explain natural selection. Like any other animal, giraffes differ genetically from one another, there is always diversity within the species. And when there is competition for food, when there is resource constraint, then that resource constraint becomes the cause for a certain evolutionary development. In the case of giraffes, the leaves on the trees went up which enabled some long-necked giraffes to have more food. They would eat more, live longer and have more offspring. So in the next generation, there were more long-necked giraffes. Over generations, the average length of the giraffe neck is increased.

This is how natural selection operates. There is diversity in any species, and there are resource constraints in the environment. There is competition within. Those who get more food are more successful in reproduction. They will have more offspring which means that by the next generation the frequency of the trait that is advantageous will increase.

How might natural selction have worked in the case of women? Originally, women were of different heights more or less like men. But a woman who was growing relatively taller tended to be less successful in producing children. The women who were shorter could reproduce more. Over many generations, there developed pronounced differences in the heights between men and woman. The height difference facilitated the reproductive success of the species. So this anatomical difference is not due to any random factors.

Another difference between woman and man is that woman has a larger proportion of fat content in her body, and man has a larger proportion of muscle mass. Fat is simply food stored in the body. Say, there is a woman who is plump and another who is a little lean, and both of them get pregnant . There is a drought or some other constraint in food availability. Which of these two will be more successful in reproduction? The one with more fat content in the body. The leaner woman has greater chances of giving birth to a deformed or underweight child. Even if the child who inherited the lean woman's genes is born, she may not be able to survive long enough to be able to reproduce herself.

When the society is under the conditions of scarcity from time to time, what type of women will survive longer and give birth to more healthy children? The women with more fat content in their body. From the point of view of reproduction, will a woman with more fat content have an evolutionary advantage if there is no situation of scarcity? No.

Why are chubby women not currently regarded beautiful? How were the heroines in the old movies or even the goddesses in the temples? Were they slim or chubby? They used to be a little plump. Being plump was a measure of reproductive success, and so it was valued. But as a society we are no longer facing those conditions of scarcity. Food is plenty, there is no need to store it inside the body. That is why size zero is becoming fashionable. Do you see the connection between the notions of beauty and the economic condition of scarcity?

Therefore the aspect of fat versus muscle is also linked to reproductive success. A chubby woman is more likely to be reproductively successful than a slim woman. A shorter woman is more likely to be reproductively successful than a taller woman.This is how anatomical differences develop through natural selection.

There are other differences as well, like females have wider pelvises to facilitate childbirth. Males have greater grip strength, proportionately larger hearts and lungs and greater aerobic capacity (more intake of oxygen during strenuous activity). Males are capable of quick bursts of energy, it makes them superior to women in strenuous activities. Women are simply made different because they have a far more elaborate mechanism of reproduction. Which kind of woman is more reproductively successful has been the crucial factor.

3. Psychological differences

Can there be certain basic psychological differences between men and women? If bodily differences are there, would there be differences in the mental makeup too?

Now, who would have more patience between man and woman? Reproductive success means much more than delivery, children have to be reared as well. It requires the traits of caring, calmness and not being anxiety-prone. Patience is needed for child care. Did natural selection give more of it to women? Are girls more caring and less aggressive by birth, compared to boys?

What calls for reproductive success is not only a certain type of body, it has to do with both the body and the mind. And the mind is closely connected to the body. The mind is so much a function of certain chemical processes happening inside the brain.

Suppose you are depressed, the doctor gives you a drug, and you might feel happy and elated. You will be surprised how a small chemical can make so much difference to your state of mind. But that is how it is. Chemicals in the body constantly affect the mind. The body generates chemicals. We must not think that the body is inherited and the mind is what the environment and socialisation have produced. Mind and body are deeply connected.

Now let us go through some studies done on this particular issue. The most consistent difference between boys and girls has been found in the area of aggression. Boys try to hurt others more frequently than girls do. In the Six Cultures Project , an extensive comparative study of children's behavior showed this difference in aggression in ages as early as three to six years. Research was carried out on children in Kenya, Mexico, India, the Philippines, Okinawa in Japan, and the US (B.B.Whiting and Edwards, 1973). A more recent cross-cultural comparison of four other cultures (the Logoli of Kenya, Nepal, Belize and American Samoa) support the finding that boys are generally more aggressive (R.L.Muroe et al, 2000).

Before the age of six years, it is not that there is no socialisation at all but it is much less. Socialisation may begin even with months-old infants. But when you are going to an early stage of life in your research, you are taking into consideration the fact that the amount of socialisation is lower then.

Even between three to six years of age, girls show more nurturance. Nurturance means helping and taking care. Girls also seem more to conform to adults' wishes, while boys try to dominate. Why is this difference? It is because of the aggression level. If there are aggression differences between boys and girls, then that is enough to create differences in many other aspects of their behaviour.

Boys tend to play in large groups, girls in smaller groups. Why so? It is found that girls prefer intimacy. Boys seem to maintain more personal distance between each other than girls do. Girls tend to be intimate, they talk about many personal things; boys less so. Other studies also show that there are inherited psychological differences between boys and girls.

The conclusion is that there are inherent psychological differences and socialisation amplifies these differences. This leads to big gender differences. The original biological differences between the genders reinforced by socialisation become bigger gender differences. But why should socialisation accentuate those differences? Boys may have somewhat more aggressive tendencies biologically but why should the society accentuate them? Girls may have somewhat less aggressive tendencies, but why should the society discourage them?

4. Gender roles

Roles that are culturally assiged to the genders are called **gender roles**. What boys are expected to do and what girls are expected to do are their gender roles.

Girls are expected to take care of their families. Why are women expected to take care of their families? Why not men? Some functions of child care, including breast feeding, can be done only by women. Some may be done by men. But if work has to be divided between the genders, child care-related activities would mostly go to the women.

If the woman is expected to take care of the children, what kind of social conditioning should be given to her? Should aggression be encouraged in her or should it be discouraged? Socialisation happens according to the roles expected from the boys and the girls. . It is preparation for certain adult duties as men and women.

For most of the the history, sex automatically led to reproduction. Only in the modern times, sex could be delinked from reproduction. In the olden days, women would give birth to many children – some of these children dying early. A woman would give birth to many children, each child being taken care of for some years. Child-bearing, rearing and many such things became the most important activities for a woman. She might do other things, but she did them in addition to the child care. Man did not have direct child care responsibilities.

Men and women may be equal in their capacities concerning many general activities, but when afamily specialises, how will it specialise? Child care function is assigned to the women – in addition to whatever else she can do. The child care function led to different type of socialisation happening between boys and girls.

What is socialisation? **Socialisation** refers to the development, through the direct and indirect influence of parents and others, of children's pattern of behaviour (and attitudes and values) that conform to the cultural expectations. Gender roles are inculcated in boys and girls through socialisation.

A girl will become a mother, a boy will become a father. Socialisation is a training process. When gender roles are fixed, socialisation will take place correspondingly. If you are writing an exam, your preparation will be corresponding to the exam, so is socialisation. If a boy has to be a father, he will be trained in some skills. If a girl has to be a mother, she will be trained in a different set of skills.

Terms

1. Sexual differencesrefer to the typical differences between females and males that are most likely due to biological differences.

2. Gender differencesrefer to differences between females and males that reflect cultural expectations and experiences.

3. Sexual dimorphism refers to a marked difference in size and appearance between the males and the females of a species.

4. Natural selection refers to the outcome of the processes that affect the frequencies of traits in a particular environment. Traits that enhance survival and reproductive success increase in frequency over time.

5. Gender roles refer to the roles that are culturally assigned to the genders.

6. Socialisation refers to the development, through the direct and indirect influence of parents and others, of children's pattern of behaviour (and attitudes and values) that conform to cultural expectations.

Think on it

1. What is the difference between sex and gender?

2. Define sexual dimorphism.

3. Explain natural selection.

4. Explain why women are shorter than men.

5. Why is fat more important to women than men?

6. Is it true that economic conditions influence notions of beauty?

7. How is man better suited to a strenuous activity?

8. Are boys by nature more aggressive? Explain.

9. Are girls by nature more caring? Explain.

10. Why is child care assigned to women only?

11. List physical as well as psychological differences between boys and girls.

12. What methods are used to find out whether the differences between boys and girls are inherited or not?

13. Why are boys socialised differently from girls?

14. Define socialisation.

• 83 •

CHAPTER TEN

Gender Hierarchy

What is the difference between gender difference and gender hierarchy? Gender difference merely suggests that men and women are different; there is no suggestion of who is more or who has more.

Gender hierarchy means unequal relationship between the sexes. All societies are characterised by gender hierarchy. Men have always dominated women. There is no society, past or present, where women on the whole were in a dominant position. There is variation, from one society to another and from one age to another, only in the degree of male domination.

We talk about patriarchy even in the context of our modern soceity. Patriarchy is a universal phenomenon. Patriarchy refers to rule by the male family heads. There is a word like 'matriarchy', rule by female heads. But there has been no society in the history of humanity, as far as we know, where matriarchy prevailed. Matriarchy therefore is only a hypothetical concept. But some history books refer to it, which is only due to a confusion between matriarchy and matriliny.

Matriliny is not the same thing as matriarchy. In a matriliny, women stay together and men join their wives after their marriage, as opposed to a patriliny where women join their husbands. But even in a women-based household, the brothers assume the authority, just as the husbands do in a patriliny.

If a society is matrilineal then the woman's position is better than in a typical patriarchical society, but still is not equal to that of a man. Woman's position in a matriliny is better only compared to her position in a patriliny. All things considered – economic, political, matrilineal, patrilineal – gender hierarchy is a universal phenomenon in human societies.

1. Hierarchy is universal

Gender hierarchy is prevalent in every society, but to what extent is a matter of many variables related to that society. Male domination is universal, but the degree of it is culture-specific.

A mother is bound to her children much more than a father. A woman is tied up, but a man is free – herein lies the essential difference. A man can freely go out, but whatever a woman wants to do, she has to do it in addition to taking care of her children and family. Man has much less social constraint compared to a woman.

Man goes out and earns, which leads to woman's economic dependence on man and this is the key factor that gives rise to a hierarchy. The mere difference in the activities both do gives rise to a hierarchical position because woman is tied to childbearing and rearing much more intimately than man.

Does it look sensible? We must examine this carefully. We are discussing at a fundamental level. Put differently, do you think that man is dependent on a woman for upkeep of his children? Or a woman is dependent on man for the upkeep of her children? We must be very careful in answering this question.

One more related question is: who is more closely connected to children, man or woman? Woman. A woman is less likely to think that she is taking care of his children. A woman is biologically and emotionally tied to her children much more than a man is to his children. She also needs somebody to take care of herself and the children. This gives rise to woman's dependence on man, it gives rise to the hierarchy. Any society is a product of a particular type of economy and a political system. When a society is such that the women depend less on the men economically, the hierarchical gap between man and woman will be less. When there is more dependence, there is more hierarchy. Dependence is the basis of the universality of hierarchy, but the type of economy and polity of a society determine the extent of the hierarchy.

2. Economic factors

Let us now examine the economic factors. We will look at some basic economic systems to estimate women's contribution in them. The more the women contribute, the less the hierarchy.

What is a woman's position in intensive agriculture? Do men dominate or do they not? There is a very clear domination. Who ploughs? It's men. Who manages the oxen? Who manages the carts? Again men. Who goes out for trading? Who does record-keeping? Who reads and writes? Women are kept more illiterate than men. In a typical society based on intensive agriculture, men clearly dominate over women.

Another word for gender hierarchy is gender stratification. Gender stratification became more pronounced in early societies based on intensive agriculture, because man was contributing more to the economy than woman. The woman did part-time agricultural work besides her household work, while the man was managing everything else.

What would be the division of work in a society of hunter-gatherers? Who is more likely to hunt and who to gather? Men hunted and women gathered. Why should it be like that? the woman has to take care of the child and she can do that while gathering but not while hunting. Not so much because man is stronger than woman.When it comes to physical strength, it is not true that men are stronger than women in every way. Men have more muscular strength, but when it comes to stamina, men seem better in releasing quick bursts of energy while women are capable of more sustained release of energy. Between men and women who work more on the whole? It's women. Who end up living longer? Women.

We need to drop the popular notion that men are stronger and women are weaker. In an athletic race man performs better, in sports man performs better, because man is more efficient at releasing quick bursts of energy. Woman is different. It is not that men are stronger and so they hunt while women can't hunt. Women too can hunt, but it wouldn't be easy for them to do that while taking care of children. The most important thing in determining the division of labour has been childcare compatibility. The woman is always expected to take care of the children in addition to everything else she does. So hunting is difficult, while gathering can be carried out even when she is taking her children along with her.

Hunting requires quick release of energy and man is better at that, but the primary thing is that hunting is not childcare-compatible. Even today, who are more likely to be chefs, men or women? It's men. But who do most of the cooking at home? Women. Why is it like that? Why don't women become chefs when they can be particularly good at it? It is because becoming a chef requires specialised training and intensive work. It also means going out, staying away from home for long hours. Men excel as chefs because they take it like any other job.

Among hunter-gatherers, men's contribution to economy is not very high. This is because though men go for hunting, their hunting may not be successful. The quantity of food they bring home is unpredictable. Gathering yields more predictable amount of food. Woman's contribution to primary subsistence in hunting and gathering societies is significant. Foraging socieities do not have high levels of gender hierarchy as compared to societies with intensive agriculture. The women in societies with horticulture are better placed compared to the women in societies with intensive agriculture because of their higher contribution to primary subsistence.

Marvin Harris discusses how plough, in the place of hoe, contributed to gender hierarchy. Hoe is a simple tool, it can be used by women. In places where the soil doesn't get hardened, a hoe is used for cultivation. Women play a role in cultivation and this has been the case in West Africa, whereas in a country like India, plough is used and women are less involved in primary subsistence. And from the plough, the need for the oxen came. Then came the cart. The technology of wheel enabled the cart. Then came trade. Then writing and education. This is what happened. It is said that plough is the enemy of woman.

The plough gave an advantage to men and that advantage added to other things. Minor differences can add up over a long period of time to create a major difference.

In an economy where woman contributes more, gender hierarchy is less. Women are contributing more now, so gender hierarchy is getting reduced. The woman is free to the extent she contributes to the economy.

If women were regarded as considerably inferior to men in one particular stage of history, it does not mean that they have always been that way. The woman's position in the society is largely a function of the economic system. And the economic system is greatly influenced by the level of technology. Hence gender relations are influenced by the state of technology. The more technologically advanced we become, the less the gender gap.

In a modern economy, the service sector, as opposed to the manufacturing sector, helps women more. Manufacturing requires some muscle power but it is irrelevant in the service sector. Service sector also provides more flexibility in working conditions. The more gender-friendly a technology is, the more it helps in lessening gender hierarchy.

3. Role of warfare

Another very important factor in determining the degree of gender hierarchy is warfare. Who would be the principal participants in warfare, men or women? Men, because they can go out to fight. They can be trained. It was found that wherever a society was engaged in warfare, the position of men in it was very high, even among hunter-gatherers.

In a study made on 33 hunting-gathering societies, the societies that engaged in warfare had positive correlation with subordination of the women (Brian Hayden, 1986). Warfare takes place due to competition over resources and is widely prevalent in human societies.

Between food and security of life, the latter takes precedence. Women's contribution to the economy plays lesser role in comparison to men's contribution to safety and survival. If a band is attacked and the men get killed, the women will be captured and taken away.

Villages, which means settled life, are possible at a foraging stage, when the fish is abundant. Just as there can be fight between bands, there can be fight between villages. When there are regular fights between one band and another band, or between one village and another village, then there is more gender hierarchy in that society. Because there is more dependence on the men.

When intensive agriculture develops, states emerge. There would be an army consisting of professional soldiers. All men need not be involved in fighting. In states, only few men, selected professionally, fight wars. Such a scenario contributes less to gender hierarchy. Warfare contributes more to gender hierarchy in primitive societies where women depend upon their husbands for their own protection.

Men have to distance themselves from their families for long periods of time while being part of an army. In some cases, such prolonged absence may even create matriliny. What will happen to woman's position then? It improves. This is what has happened in the case of Nairs in Kerala. Men were taking part in long-distance wars, and women were left in the villages. A household would be led by just one man. Such social systems contributed to the empowerment of women.

4. Matriliny of Khasi

The Khasi of Meghalaya follow matrilineal descent. The ancestral property goes from the mother to the youngest daughter. The system of residence is uxorilocal. Men have no inheritance rights.

The Meghalaya Succession Act of 1986 conferred Khasi and Jaintiya men the right to dispose their self-acquired property by will. Previously these men did not have such a right. The Khasi custom prescribes the devolution of all property exclusively in the female line.

While women are central to the family in Khasi traditions, they need to be guarded by men. The Khasi say, 'War and politics for men, property and children for women'. Only men attend the traditional village and state councils.

The youngest daughter of a family has the responsibility to take care of her parents. She is also expected to help the members of her matri-kin if they suffer any misfortune. But she has little say in the control and the management of the property. It is her mother's brother who enjoys these privileges.

It is the women who have to ensure that religious rites on occasions such as someone's death are conducted properly. But they seek the assistance of their male matri-kin in this. Priesthood is a male vocation.

There are inherent contradictions in matrilineal systems. The inheritance line does not match with the authority line. The man faces dilemmas, his children vs. his sister's children, his wife vs. his sister. Consanguineal ties are emphasised over affinal ties.

The man lives in his wife's house but may not feel like he belongs there, he has no rights over property and has limited control over his own children. At the same time, he is expected to protect and provide for his family. This may generate role conflicts. The men couldn't pass on their self-acquired property to their sons till recently. Even the women have role conflicts in this system. A woman may blame her husband for not doing enough for her, and she may also blame her brother for not doing enough for her.

Collective conversion to Christianity weakened matriliny in Meghalaya. The father's authority is growing. Men have been the first to get educated and get employment, with their position improving.

Think on it

1. How is gender hierarchy different from gender difference?

2. Is matriarchy only a hypothesis?

3. Is patriarchy a universal phenomenon? Explain.

4. What is the most important factor that influences gender-based division of labour?

5. Was gender hierarchy high among the foragers?

6. Did gender hierarchy increase when economy moved from extensive agriculture to intensive agriculture? Explain.

7. How does plough contribute to gender hierarchy?

8. Does service economy dilute gender hierarchy?

9. How does warfare contribute to gender hierarchy?

10. Why may warfare not increase gender hierarchy in a state?

11. Can warfare contribute to matriliny? Explain

12. Identify the kinds of role conflict that Khasi society produces.

CHAPTER ELEVEN

Marriage

Let us ask ourselves an important question: why do human societies have marriage at all? **Marriage**refers to socially approved sexual and economic union, usually between a man and a woman, that is presumed, both by the couple and by others, to be more or less permanent, and that subsumes reciprocal rights and obligations between the two spouses and their future children.

It is extremely rare to find a society that has no marriage. The Na people of China and the Nayars of Kerala are two such exceptions. The Nayars do not constitute a society, they are a caste. Barring these exceptions, we can consider marriage as a universal phenomenon.

1. Why marriage?

Why should marriage be universal? Why didn't any alternative arrangements happen in any society? We can think of men and women living together, having children, and all the children being taken care of by the adults in a communal living. Or since the bond between the woman and her children is a particularly strong one, women and their children could constitute the families, while men could take care of all the women and all the children in the commune. Why weren't there any societies with communal living like this?

Why should it be one man, one woman and their children within the marriage framework? Since it is sex that leads to reproduction and not marriage, what is the need for a man-woman bond as in a marriage? That is the question. Besides the basic bond between mother and children, why should there be a permanent bonding between man and woman or between father and children?

Do societies have marriage to prevent incest which may lead to the birth of children with abnormalities? But even without marriage, a brother and a sister can know that they are siblings. So if avoidance of sex between siblings is made a cultural norm. incest can be avoided even in a society without marriage. Knowledge of who is one's own mother is enough to avoid incest.

What if closely related people have sex? Actually that may not be a problem. In southern India, there has been a long tradition of cross cousin marriages, and among Muslims, parallel cousin marriages have been a tradition. The only universal rule is: no sex between siblings, brother and sister, born to same parents.

One argument for the universality of marriage could be that when a woman is beautiful, a man would want to have her for himself alone, which means marrying her. But if a woman is beautiful, then many men would want her, in which case not marrying her to any one man is better for all the men that desire her. So marriage decreases sexual rivalry. A society without marriage is promiscuous. Promiscuity may increase the totality of sex which may be good.

The mother feels naturally responsible towards her children, as she gave birth to them. The mother-child bond is not simply cultural, it is biological. We see the mother-child bond in all kinds of animals living around us – in dogs, cats, chicken etc.

The mother-child bond among humans is very strong. Culture may reinforce that, but there is enough biological basis for it to exist. Mother is in control of her children. All men are taking care of all the children. It means there is a family. **Family** is a social and economic unit consisting minimally of a parent and a child. There can be a family without marriage.

Family is nothing but a unit of parents and children, there need be no marriage. Marriage is about male-female bonding. Women are intrinsically connected to their children but men are relatively free.

One point that is put forth in explaining the marriage system is that every woman is assured of a partner through marriage, so it brings equality between the attractive women and the unattractive women. However, we rejected equality in so many other areas, where are we pursuing equality at all? People have not been treated equally in any society. We have always ignored the poor. Therefore, we can't say societies devised marriage to help the less desirable women.

Another argument could be that if all the men were made responsible for all the children, then most of the men will end up becoming irresponsible. A man has to be allotted some children for him to assume real responsibility. Let us see some possible justification for this reasoning. Among hunter-gatherers, land is held in common. There is no individual allotment because hunter-gatherers depend on the entire ecosystem. In pastoralism, the land is common but animals are privately owned. Private ownership of animals may lead to better care of them rather than all the animals being taken care of by all the people.

Now, if children have to be allotted to men, could it not be done randomly? Or should more children be given to some men who are more efficient? But why random, why not make a man responsible only to his own children? And a man can know his own children if we avoid promiscuity and go for marriage.

That surely is a possibility – marriage could have been brought in to allot children to their likely fathers and it could have evolved naturally to a system where the men are the real fathers for sure. This approach is superior to communal living and more effective in the management of children, and there is more involvement of human emotion.

This is a line of reasoning to arrive at the most probable thing that might have created the marriage system. But how should anthropologists find out what might have actually happened? Anthropology studies not only human societies, it studies those of other species too. And anthropologists wanted to investigate if something like a marriage takes place in any species other than human.

Do birds get married? Marriage here means male-female bonding , and doesn't imply any weddings. What are all the animals that are getting married? Anthropologists wanted to find out where all there is male female bonding. There is mother-children bond in many species. There are families in many species. It seemed like marriage is relatively rare across the species.

Anthropologists wanted to find out empirically why marriage happens in human societies, and they started examining animal species. It was found that many birds and some mammals are getting married. That was the first news. The second news is that marriage is there wherever female, for some time, is not able to take care of its offspring. This is called the postpartum feeding problem.

In whichever species the female is not in a position to fully take care of her offspring, she is going for marriage. Whose need is marriage? Who is going for marriage? It is not the male, it is the female. And what is her need? Her need for a male is not coming from her physical weakness, but from her responsibility to take care of her offspring. Even if she was as strong as man, she would depend on man because she becomes vulnerable for some time after pregnancy. She becomes vulnerable at a crucial stage of nurturing her offspring. She has to feed her children and not just herself. So what does she do? She cultivates a male partner. That's how this business of marriage started.

Experts had postulated various reasons for marriage such as sexual competition, division of labour, and child care, but those theories did not correlate with empirical findings. Only when one factor is considered – the postpartum feeding problem – the correlation showed up. This is an empirical finding. In whichever species the female is in a position to take care of her children adequately without any problem, she is not going for marriage.

The female monkey goes around carrying her child with her. The kangaroo too does the same. In some species, the offspring is born with enough maturity, as in horses, and the young ones can take care of themselves. Marriages are not seen in all these species.

In the case of a human infant, it depends on the mother for a long period of time and the mother cannot be as productive during that phase as she could be at other times. Without enough food, her nourishment will suffer, her children's nourishment will suffer. Out of her helplessness, she is making this offer and man is falling for it. This has been empirically verified.

Anthropologists have come to the conclusion that the postpartum feeding problem is the essential reason for marriage. When did this problem arise in the human species? For a long time, the early humans had a lot of body hair, just like chimpanzees. When a female had thick body hair, she was in a better position to carry her child. Then at some stage, the early humans lost the thick body hair. In addition, they took to hunting. Both these developments contributed to male female bonding. A woman can't hunt while engaged in child care. She found it convenient to have a man. This is the account given in Ember & Ember regarding the origins of human marriage.

So the Homo sapiens did not invent marriage as society and culture developed. The Homo sapiens were born into a culture of both family and marriage. There are around forty species among birds and mammals where male-female bonding exists, correlating with the postpartum feeding problem. This shows woman needing man's help is an important factor in creating human societies such as ours.

Now we can understand what the bases of marriage are. Post-partum feeding problem is the very basis of the marriage. And there are other factors too: division of labour between the sexes and socialisation of children.

In the contemporary times, women are clearly becoming less dependent. Sometimes the woman is in a position to say to the man: 'I don't need you for the sake of my children. If you love me, you can be around. Otherwise, thank you.' So the foundational reason for marriage is gradually weakening as women become more independent and secure.

We can often see among our own families and the people around us that the stronger relationship within the family is between the mother and the children and not between the father and the children. The bond between the female and her offspring has a strong biological foundation. The bond between the male and his offspring is brought about by the institution of marriage. In modern legal systems too, mothers are usually given more rights in relation to their children.

2. Incest taboo

Just as marriage is nearly universal, incest taboo too is nearly universal. **Incest taboo** refers to prohibition of sexual intercourse between mother and son, father and daughter, and brother and sister; It often extends to other relatives.

Only rarely is this taboo not observed. Incan and Hawaiian royal families allowed marriage within the family. They did not want to give their daughters to commoners. Egyptian aristocracy too disregarded the taboo. In ancient Egypt, between 30 BC and 324 AD, it is estimated that around 8% of commoner marriages were between brothers and sisters. Except for such rare examples, the incest taboo is universal.

Anthropologists have pondered on the basis of the incest taboo. The basic reason seems to be that incest leads to inbreeding which causes serious health problems. It has been found that simple societies are aware of this. When might they have learnt about the ill cffccts of inbreeding? It could have been a long time ago. By the time anthropologists started making observations, they did not find any society that did not have this taboo. It is possible that societies without this taboo might have gone extinct a long time ago.

It is not necessary that a society should be aware of the adverse consequences of not having the incest taboo. Any society that was not aware of it would have been eliminated long ago. If societies don't observe the taboo, natural selection will eliminate them, because inbreeding leads to weak and sick children. William

Durham's cross-cultural study (1991) found that the biological harm to the offspring being the cause for the taboo was known in 50% of the societies that were studied.

But how does one explain the inbreeding royal families producing healthy children? An example of such a healthy person would be the world-beauty of antiquity, Cleopatra. She was the progeny of brother-sister mating and this inbreeding went on for several successive generations before her. How did such royal families survive the ill effects of inbreeding?

It turns out that inbreeding is harmful only when there are lethal genes in a clan. These lethal genes tend to be recessive. A recessive gene implies that unless it is on both the chromosomes coming from the father side and the mother side, it would not be expressed. If the gene is dominant then it will be expressed even if it is there on the chromosome coming from one side. People with dominant lethal genes would not survive long enough to pass on their genes.

When is inbreeding harmful? It is harmful when a society has some recessive lethal genes spread across the population. When closely related people marry and both of them have the lethal genes in recessive condition, their child can get the gene in the chromosomes inherited from both the sides, and then it will be expressed. The child gets the disease. If a lethal gene is coming from one parent and the same lethal gene is not coming from the other parent, then the child may have the gene only on one chromosome; he will not get the disease. Closed marriages increase the frequency of lethal genes getting expressed. Why were not the royal families eliminated because of inbreeding? It's because they did not have any lethal genes running in their lineages.

Anthropologists now think that inbreeding is the most important reason for the incest taboo. Some studies show the rates of abnormalities in uncle-niece marriages (which is allowed in some societies) are high.

Besides inbreeding, some anthropologists gave other cultural reasons for the incest taboo. E.B. Tyler said that the incest taboo allows a society to send women to other groups, which leads to cooperation between the groups. The taboo contributes to cooperation across groups . This theory is further elaborated by Claude Lévi Strauss. But if giving out helps, some women can be given out, why should there be a general taboo? So there are other explanations. Malinowski said incest taboo came about to avoid sexual competition within the family. But how can a marriage between a grown-up brother and sister generate rivalry at all?

Edward Westermarck says that familiarity leads to lack of sexual interest. If those familiar from childhood are married, it may not lead to successful marriage. There is some evidence for this argument. Arthur Wolf's study of some Chinese communities in Taiwan found that the custom of 'raising the daughter-in-law from childhood' is associated with sexual disinterest and higher divorce rates. Studies by Yonina Talmon found that children reared together in the kibbutzim of Israel have avoided marriage as well as sexual relations among themselves.

The childhood-familiarity theory of Westermarck may explain why marriage is not preferred, but it does not explain the taboo itself. Neither Malinowski's family-disruption theory nor Tyler's co-operation theory may explain the why of such a strong taboo. Inbreeding theory offers a better explanation for the near universality of the taboo – by placing it in the interests of the very survival of the group.

Incest taboo is here defined as prohibition of sex within the nuclear family – except between the parents. The universality of the incest taboo is about the taboo within the nuclear family. But the incest taboo can go beyond the nuclear family. It can be extended to some people outside the nuclear family, depending on the culture. Can a Hindu marry his parallel cousin? No. **Parallel cousins** refer to the children of the siblings of the same sex. One's parallel cousins are the father's brothers' children and the mother's sisters' children. A Hindu can't marry his parallel cousin. Can a Muslim marry? Yes. It is a tradition among the Muslims.

Can a North Indian Hindu marry his cross cousin? No. **Cross cousins** refer to the children of the siblings of the opposite sex.

One's cross-cousins are the father's sisters' children and the mother's brothers' children. But cross cousin marriages are an age-old tradition in South India. A parallel cousin is taken as one's own brother or sister among the Hindus, but this is not true for the Muslims. And in North India, even cross cousins are regarded in the same way as parallel cousins. In South India, a cross cousin is favored as a mate.

The incest taboo is nearly universal within the nuclear family. Extension of the taboo beyond the nuclear family is also universal, but to whom it is extended is determined by the culture. One of the things anthropologists would like to know is how and why this taboo was extended. One can explain the incest taboo within the nuclear family from a biological viewpoint but the other extensions only from a cultural point of view.

3. Nayars and definition of marriage

Marriage is defined as a socially recognised sexual and economic union between a man and a woman with rights and obligations, towards each other and towards their children. However, marraige among the Nayars does not satisfy this definition.

The Nayars live in Kerala, and they are an example of a matrilineal society. Among the Nayars there is no such thing as marriage as we know it. Or at least, it was so traditionally. How was it like with them then? Here we give an account of the Nayars as they were over 200 years ago, when the British were assuming control in Indian states.

There was no permanent bond between a man and a woman. A woman did not have a proper husband. She had what were called visiting husbands. When the woman became pregnant, one of the visiting husbands would give her a gift. There was nothing more to it. It was not a very big gift for the purpose of the upbringing of the child, but just a small gift. None of these husbands had any responsibility towards the woman or towards her children. They would visit the woman and go. But where was the marriage then?

Nayar girls did marry. There is a marriage ceremony when the boy ties the tali, after which they would spend three days together and then they would part. It was over, mostly. That husband did not have any further role in the girl's life. Only if he died at some point of time, this woman would observe the death rituals. The boy belonged to a particular lineage. Girls from a certain lineage had to pick up husbands only from a specified lineage. Marriages of all girls from a certain lineage were done in a group marriage ceremony. The girls were typically prepubescent, aged between 7 and 12.

The lineages among the Nayars were hierarchical. A woman could have a visiting husband from a higher lineage or from one that was equal to her own, but not from a lower lineage. She could have a visiting husband from a higher caste. Suppose she was pregnant and no visiting husband gave her a gift, then it signified a suspicion that she had a relation with somebody from a lower lineage or a lower caste. She could even be ostracised for that. Even worse, she could even be sold as a slave. Sometimes, she could even be killed along with her child. The Nayars went to extreme lengths to retain the purity of the lineage.

There was no restriction on the number of the visiting husbands a woman could have. Some could visit regularly, some might rarely. There also wasn't any limit on how many women a Nayar man could visit.

The men of Namboodari Brahmins could go as visiting husbands to the women from the higher lineages of Nayars. They also became ritual husbands to the women from the highest lineages of Nayars. These Brahmins had normal families of their own and they had this kind of relationship only with the Nayars. A Nayar woman might think of some of these Brahmins as her husbands, but these same Brahmins did not regard the Nayar women as their wives, because no marriage happened between them according to the Vedic rites. The Brahmins' perspective of what was going on was different from the Nayars' perspective.

How did this system of man-woman relations develop among the Nayars? The Nayar men used to go to participate in long-distance warfare. Normally when the men stayed far away from their people, then it could foster matrilocality and matrilineality in a community. The unusual thing in Nayars' case is not simply matrilineality but absence of marriage.

Kathleen Gough says marriage should be defined differently if that definition has to be universally valid, including for the Nayars. She offers this different definition: "Marriage is a relationship established between a woman and one or more other persons which provides that a child born to the woman under circumstances not prohibited by the rules of the relationship is accorded full birth-status rights common to normal members of his society or social stratum." So, marriage is something that gives legitimacy to a child according to this definition.

Should we change the definition of marriage, as Kathleen Gough suggests, or should we stick to the original definition and say that the Nayars are an exception? Normally, we don't have to define anything in such a way that every single instance of it is covered. One can also say the standard definition of marriage is true of all societies in general, and the Nayars do not constitute a society, they are only a section of a society.

The way man-woman relations existed among the Nayars shows in what strange ways a group of people could live in a society. For a woman, a hypogamous union was something that invited punishment, excommunication, and even a brutal death, but having a large number of husbands was very normal.

How was marriage actually seen in the Nayar community? Much before or around the time of puberty, a girl was married to a boy and the two of them spent 3 nights together and then they separated. There was nothing more to it. The boy was just a ritual husband. Later, if he died first, the practice of ritual pollution would be observed by the woman. The marriage in a way gave approval for the woman to have sex with others. It was a legitimisation of sex. It also gave her the status of a person entitled to reproduction. If she gave birth to a child, he or she was accepted as a member of the community with full status. That's why after considering the

Nayars, Kathleen Gough made legitimisation of the child the central element of marriage.

Legitimisation of a child among the Nayaras required adherence to certain rules. For example, one woman could not have two visiting husbands who were brothers or from the same property-holding group. One man could not be a visiting husband to two women from the same family. While there was much freedom in the choice of sexual partners, there were a number of restrictions too. The restrictions were concerned with exogamy, endogamy and incest.

Although the visiting husbands did not take care of their wives, it was not that men as such were not contributing. Men contributed to their families as brothers and uncles and not as husbands and fathers.

In her definition, Gough says, marriage is "a relationship established between a woman and one or more other persons." She does not say 'between a woman and one or more men', she says 'one or more persons'. By this, Gough wants to cover woman-woman marriages also.

Take the Nandi, a pastoral society from Kenya. Among them, female-female marriages make up about 3% of marriages. If a woman does not produce sons, her share of property will go to the sons of her co-wives or her husband's brother. In such a situation, she could marry another woman, who will have sex with other men to have children. And the children so born will be considered the children of this female. She will now be entitled to her share of the property. The female husband is regarded as a man, she would even dress like a man, so she can no longer have sex with her former husband.

Some societies are not concerned about the legitimacy of the children as much as it used to be the case among the Nayars. Among the Kadar of Nigeria, children born from premarital pregnancies are accepted as members of the patrilineage. Most marriages in this tribe result from infant betrothals. So, Kathleen Gough's definition of marriage as the source of legitimacy to the children fails to cover the types of marriages in some societies.

There are a lot of different types of marriages in human societies. Different rules for men and women living together exist across societies. According to Marvin Harris, one need not define marriage on a single criterion like the legitimacy of the children.

Terms

1. **Marriage**refers to socially approved sexual and economic union, usually between a man and a woman, that is presumed, both by the couple and by others, to be more or less permanent, and that subsumes reciprocal rights and obligations between the two spouses and their future children.

2. **Family** is a social and economic unit consisting minimally of a parent and a child.

3. **Incest taboo** refers to prohibition of sexual intercourse between mother and son, father and daughter, and brother and sister; often extends to other relatives.

4. **Parallel cousins** refer to children of siblings of the same sex. One's parallel cousins are the father's brothers children and the mother's sisters' children.

5. **Cross cousins** refer to children of siblings of the opposite sex. One's cross-cousins are the father's sisters' children and mother's brothers' children.

6. **Hypergamy**: marriage of a woman with a man of higher social status.

7. **Hypogamy**: marriage of a woman with a man of lower socials status.

Think on it

1. Define marriage.

2. Can families be possible without marriages?

3. Are there communities without marriage?

4. Does marriage lead to more efficient way of taking care of the children?

5. What is the role of the postpartum feeding problem in the development of marriage?

6. Do all primates have marriages? If not, why so?

7. How is the incest taboo defined?

8. What is the biological reason advanced to explain the incest taboo?

9. What are the cultural reasons given to explain the incest taboo?

10. Is the incest taboo extended beyond nuclear family? Give examples.

11. Who were the visiting husbands among the Nayars? What were their rights and duties?

12. Under what circumstances a new-born child would not be accepted by the Nayars?

13. What is Kathleen Gough's definition of marriage?

14. Why are there many woman-woman marriages among the Nandi?

CHAPTER TWELVE

Types of Marriage

1. Preferential marriages

Marriage rules specify the group within which one should marry as well as the groups one should avoid. **Exogamy** is the rule specifying marriage to a person from outside one's own group (kin or community). **Endogamy** is the rule specifying marriage to a person within one's own group (kin, caste, community). For Hindus, caste is an endogamous unit and gotram is an exogamous unit.

Within the limits of exogamy and endogamy, marriage rules allow some preferences to be made in mate selection. **Preferential marriages** refer to marriage rules that are expressed as preferences rather than requirements or prescriptions. Many societies favour their men and women having certain preferences in the selection of a mate.

In South India, cross cousins are preferred as husbands and wives. Marrying a patri cross cousin means a man marrying the father's sister's daughter. Marrying a matri cross cousin means a man marrying the mother's brother's daughter. If a boy is marrying a patri-cross cousin, can't the same marriage be called matri-cross from the girl's point of view? No. Patri-cross and matri-cross are defined from the male point of view.

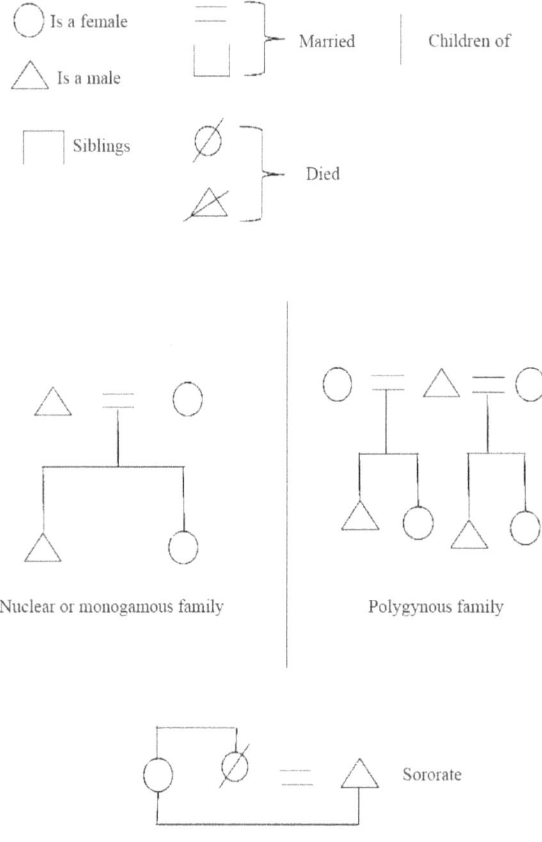

Fig. 12.1: Kinship diagrams

They are named from the viewpoint of the male ego. **Ego**is the reference point or focal person in the reckoning of kinship. If a society allows patri-cross marriage, it does not automatically mean that it allows matri-cross too.

There are preferences in the secondary marriages too. **Sororate** refers to a custom whereby a woman is obliged to marry her deceased sister's husband. What can one make of a practice like this? It is a woman occupying the position of her dead sister, she will be taking care of her sister's children and her sister's husband. This shows a woman is replaceable and is being replaced by her sister.

Under sororate, a woman will fulfil her dead sister's responsibilities, her group will not have to return the bride price. Sororate reflects the group nature of marriage. One woman failed, in a way. The group replaces her. The emphasis is on replaceability, not on individualism. Individualism has been growing in the recent times, in general as well as in the context of marriage. This was not the case before.

Levirate refers to a custom whereby a man is obliged to marry his deceased brother's wife. The attitude is that man is replaceable. This again shows that marriage is more of a relationship between groups.

2. Polygamy

Monogamy refers to marriage between only one man and only one woman at a time. **Polygamy** refers to plural marriage where one individual is married to more than one spouse simultaneously. **Polygyny** refers to the marriage of one man to more than one woman at a time. It is a subset of polygamy.

Polygyny is practised when the sex ratio is in favour of women. It can happen due to a loss of men in warfare, or it can happen due to cultural reasons. The culture may assign higher marriageable age for men, which leads to fewer men being eligible for marriage. Long postpartum sex taboo was also assumed to be a factor in polygyny. **Postpartum sex taboo**refers to prohibition of sexual intercourse between a couple for a period of time after the birth of their child. When statistical-control analysis was applied on all the three factors mentioned above – imbalanced sex ratio in favour of women, delayed age of marriage for men, long postpartum sex taboo – it was found that the long postpartum sex taboo did not predict polygyny. So it has been ruled out as a factor. Imbalanced sex ratio and delayed age of marriage for men emerged as strong predictors. And when these two factors are combined, there is an even higher likelihood for polygyny.

Some recent studies of foraging societies suggest that those in which men control hunting or fishing territories are more likely to be polygynous (Sellen and Hruschka, 2004). But the control of gathering sites by men did not predict polygyny.

Studies by Bobby Low (1990) showed that the pathogen load in a society predicts polygyny. Healthy men are fewer, a woman may want to marry a healthy man though he is already married. A man may want to marry more than one woman to have more genetic variation among his children. Nigel Barber (2008) found that sex-ratio and pathogen stress predicted polygyny in modern nations as well.

George Peter Murdock's World Ethnographic Sample included only four societies (less than 1% of the total) in which polyandry was practised. **Polyandry** refers to the marriage of one woman to more than one man at a time.

Polyandry is a way of dealing with resource constraint. It avoids fragmentation of the property, it also checks the population growth.

Polyandry is not a mirror image of polygyny. In polygyny, a man marries more than one woman, he has power over them. In polyandry, usually, brothers bring one woman to their home. Both are patriarchal in structure.

3. Marriage payments

Data from Schlegel and Elou (1988) showed that in 75% of the societies known to anthropology, explicit economic transactions take place before or after marriage. These economic transactions, called marriage payments, may include any of these: bride price (44%), bride service (19%), gift exchange (11%), exchange of females (6%), dowry (8%), and indirect dowry (12%).

Bride price refers to substantial gift of goods or money given to the bride's kin by the groom or his kin at or before the marriage.

This practice does not reduce a woman to a slave. The bride price may be important to the woman and her family. The fee they receive can serve as a security deposit. If the marriage fails through no fault of the woman and she returns, the bride price may not be returned. Also, the woman's parents and family may pressure her to stay in the marriage because they do not want to return the bride price.

Cross-culturally, societies with the custom of bride price are likely to practise horticulture and lack any social stratification. The custom of bride price is also likely where women contribute a great deal to primary subsistence activities and where they contribute more than men to all kinds of economic activities.

Bride service refers to the work performed by the groom for his bride's family for a variable length of time either before or after the marriage. In some societies, it may last only for a few months, in others, for as long as several years. In some societies, bride service is offered as a substitute for bride price or to reduce bride price.

The societies that practise the exchange of females – like Tiv in West Africa – tend to be horticultural and egalitarian. Exchange of gifts of equal value happens more frequently than the exchange of females.

In the practices of bride price and bride service, women and money or labour move in opposite directions. In the practice of dowry, women and money move in the same direction. The woman is bringing the money. How do you explain dowry? Under what circumstances would a woman come depriving her family of her contribution and also bringing a substantial sum of money along with her?

The practice of dowry is found where women's contribution to the primary subsistence is less and where there is social stratification. It is also found only in those societies where there is monogamy. A man can marry only one woman, her economic contribution is less and there may be highly unequal families. A woman is being sent, her husband and in-laws are expected to take care of her; the financial contribution from the woman is the dowry that she brings with her.

In India, dowry has been an age-old practice. What is happening to it nowadays? Is the trend of dowry coming down or going up? It is hugely coming down. A greater contribution to the economy from women is automatically reducing the incidence of dowry.

Indirect dowry refers to goods given by the groom's kin to the bride (or her father who passes most of them to her) at or before her marriage. Dowry is provided by the bride's family to the bride and the groom. The indirect dowry comes from the groom's family. Among the Basseri of Iran, the groom's father gives cash to the bride's father, who uses most of it to buy household items for his daughter. This is a form of bride price.

4. Pahari polyandry

The system of polyandry followed by the Pahari, living in the Jausar Bawar region of Uttarakhand was described by Gerald D Berreman (1975). This type of polyandry was explained in terms of the developmental cycle of the domestic group. As we will see shortly, the system of polyandry passes through different stages – that may include monogamy, polygyny, polygynandry (group marriage)

A woman goes through a marriage ceremony with the eldest brother, all the brothers thereupon become her husbands. No brother can remain a member of a joint family claiming exclusive rights to a wife. Children recognise a group of brothers as their fathers. The custom of bride price is followed when a marriage takes place.

Women are almost as productive as men in agricultural work. With the exception of ploughing and other activities involving draft animals, they do virtually the same farm work as men. Families with less land would have fewer wives. Paternity is not clear, maternity is acknowledged and recognised though all the wives of the brothers are regarded as mothers by the children in the family. If family gets divided, the women and the children will be allotted to different brothers. Factors such as relative age, emotional involvement, marriage sequence, and physical resemblance may be taken into account in alloting the wives and children to the men.

The joint family is patrilineal and patrilocal. The marriage is a contract between a group of brothers and a woman. A man can marry many times, but a woman can't go for a new marriage without getting the existing one terminated. Children remain with fathers.

Pahari polyandry can be simply described as a group of brothers marrying one or more women. It can take different forms over the course of years in a person's life. We will look at this process through a hypothetical example.

1910 F15 = [M18, M15, M12] In the year 1910, an 18-year-old man marries a 15-year-old woman. The woman automatically becomes a wife to her husband's 15-year-old and 12-year-old brothers. This is an instance of fraternal polyandry, though the youngest one may not have sexual relations for some years yet.

1915 [F16, F20] = [M23, M20, M17] The eldest brother marries again. This arrangement now becomes a group marriage – called polygynandry – as three brothers have two common wives.

1920 [F23, F21, F25] = [M28, M25, M22] A divorcee or a widow is brought in without any wedding ceremony. In the case of a divorcee, the bride price might be paid to her previous husband. At this point, there are three men and three women in the family.

1930 [F33, F31, F35] = [M35, M32] The eldest brother dies. The wives now outnumber the husbands.

1940 [F41, F45] = [M42] When one of the wives and one more brother dies, with one man and two women alive, the marital setup becomes polygyny.

1950 [F51] = [M52] When one other wife dies, with only one man and one woman alive, the arrangement becomes a monogamy.

5. Acquiring mate

According to Madan and Majumdar, eight important ways of acquiring a mate are reported from tribal India.

Marriage by bride price. The Nagas and the tribes of Middle India practise this. When the bride price is too high, the man could resort to marriage by capture.

Marriage by service is resorted to when the bride price is high. If a Gond or a Baiga male finds himself in a position where he is unable to pay the bride price, he goes to serve in the woman's house. It is reported that the Gurkhas from Nepal come to serve among the Khasa and after some years of service they get to marry the women.

Marriage in exchange refers to households exchanging women with each other. This avoids bride price and bride service. This is found among various tribes all over India.

Probationary marriage. Among the Kuki, the man stays in the woman's house for weeks. If they get along, then they get married, otherwise the man leaves paying cash compensation.

Marriage by capture was sometimes practised by the Nagas. This was reported even among the Gond, the Ho, the Bhils and several other pre-Dravidian tribes. Sometimes, mock fights takes place while the parents pretend to resist.

Marriage by trial is the recognition of courage and bravery of the man. Among the Bhils, during the Holi festival, a man attempts to break open a coconut tied to the top of a pole around which girls would be dancing while also trying to stop the man. He will choose one of the girls if he succeeds.

Marriage by elopement takes place in many tribes and the parents usually get the couple back after some days.

Marriage by intrusion is the opposite of marriage by capture. Among the Ho and the Birhor, the woman who comes to stay in the house of a man is often insulted and ill-treated, but would finally be accepted.

6. *Household and Joint Family*

Householdrefers to a social group occupying a dwelling or other domicile. Membership comprises a family or **domestic group**that may also include hired labourers and domestic servants.

The concept of household derives from British feudalism where each 'holding' of land was identified with a house and its inhabitants, which was geographically fixed and had some social permanence. It was a legal unit of ownership and was responsible for the payment of taxes. A family was based on monogamous marriage, and the head of the household was the formal representative of the unit to the higher levels in the feudal system.

Although most societies have domestic groups of some kind, they may not be equivalent to the kind the English had. Some societies have compounds that include many people, they could be pastoral nomads or foragers. And the membership of these compounds may change rapidly. In some polygynous societies, each wife has her own economic means and supports her children.

Anthropologists have a problem with the universal applicability of the concept of household. But it does apply to some societies where households are recognised as units by the people themselves. The land, the most important means of production, is owned by the household. Its members preserve the land, develop it and pass it on to the next generation. They consume as a unit and they coordinate their activities.

The concept of household was also found to be useful to anthropologists when economists developed their model for households and the anthropologists could use this data. Agricultural economists take households as bounded units that deal with the external world primarily through market. But anthropologists find households as embedded in local communities with external institutions for production and distribution. They are involved in labour-sharing, gift exchange and expensive ritual obligations. Anthropologists could never leave community-level analysis. And feminists never ignored the gender-based distribution of goods within a household.

Cyclical change refers to regular, repetitive courses of growth, decline and revival. The concept of **developmental cycle**applies the biological metaphor of the life cycle to groups rather than individuals. The most important unit to which the developmental cycle refers is the domestic group. Domestic groups are founded usually in marriage. They grow through the birth of the children and the acquisition of other dependents, and they disperse through the marriage of the children and the death of the older generation. The composition of a household is changed through the developmental cycle.

The main reason to study the cyclical pattern of growth in the study of domestic groups is that a field study describes a variety of groups at one point in time. We need to differentiate whether these are different types of groups or the same type of group at different stages.

A.M. Shah says the ideal of the joint family in India is the principle of residential unity of the patri-kin and their wives. The observance of this principle depends on the degree of Sanskritisation of a caste.

A typical joint family in any village is at a certain stage of the developmental cycle. Some joint families move in the direction of increasing size, some in the direction of decreasing size. Two or more households may hold and manage property jointly and help each other in many ways as in a single family.

A.M. Shah analysed 1820-30 census data on the household composition in a Gujarat village. It showed the average size of the household was only 4.5 and households rarely went beyond the phase of co-residence of two or more married sons during the lifetime of their parents. Ghurye's analysis of a Maharashtra village during the same time showed the average size of the household to be the same. So it can't be assumed that villagers in the traditional India lived in complex households of three to four generations. As per the 1911 census, the average population per house in India was 4.9 or much the same as in European countries.

If Sanskritisation is a variable impacting the principle of residential unity, the towns might be following this principle more than the villages. But growing Westernisation would reduce the importance of this principle.

Henry Maine went by the Hindu sacred texts that put forward the joint family as an ideal and proposed that the Indian family was different from the Western family. This Indological and textual approach to the study of the Indian society wrongly gave the impression to many that the large joint family was the empirical reality of the Indian society over the millennia.

Terms

1. **Exogamy** is the rule specifying marriage to a person from outside one's own group (kin or community).

2. **Endogamy** is the rule specifying marriage to a person within one's own group (kin, caste, community).

3. **Preferential marriages**refer to marriage rules that are expressed as preferences rather than requirements or prescriptions.

4. **Prescriptive marriages** refer to marriage rules that are obligatory rather than optional or simply preferred.

5. **Ego**is the reference point or focal person in the reckoning of kinship.

6. **Monogamy** refers to marriage between only one man and only one woman at a time.

7. **Polygamy** refers to plural marriage where one individual is married to more than one spouse simultaneously.

8. **Polygyny** refers to the marriage of one man to more than one woman at a time.

9. **Postpartum sex taboo**refers to prohibition of sexual intercourse between a couple for a period of time after the birth of their child.

10. **Polyandry** refers to the marriage of one woman to more than one man at a time.

11. **Sororal polygyny** refers to the marriage of a man to two or more sisters at the same time.

12. **Nonsororal polygyny** refers to the marriage of a man to two or more women who are not sisters.

13. Fraternal polyandry refers to the marriage of a woman to two or more brothers at the same time.

14. Nonfraternal polyandry refers to marriage of a woman to two or more men who are not brothers.

15. Bride price refers to substantial gift of goods or money given to the bride's kin by the groom or his kin at or before the marriage.

16. Bride service refers to the work performed by the groom for his bride's family for a variable length of time either before or after the marriage.

17. Dowry refers to substantial transfer of goods or money from the bride's family to the bride.

18. Indirect dowry refers to goods given by the groom's kin to the bride (or her father who passes most of them to her) at or before her marriage.

19. Sororate refers to a custom whereby a woman is obliged to marry her deceased sister's husband.

20. Levirate refers to a custom whereby a man is obliged to marry his deceased brother's wife.

21. Developmental cycle: the life-cycle of the domestic group seen as a cyclica succession of phases of expansion, dispersion or fission and replacement.

22. Household: a social group occupying a dwelling or other domicile.

Think on it

1. What is the difference between exogamy and endogamy?

2. What is a preferential marriage?

3. A boy's patri-cross cousin is a girl's matri-cross cousin. If a patri-cross cousin marriage is allowed, does it mean matri-cross cousin is also allowed?

4. What factors explain polygyny?

5. What is statistical control analysis?

6. What factors explain polyandry?

7. How is bride service different from bride price?

8. How is indirect dowry different from dowry?

9. What factors contribute to dowry?

10. How is levirate different from sororate?

11. What do levirate and sororate tell us about the meaning of marriage?

12. What is meant by developmental cycle of a family?

13. Does polyandry give power to women?.

14. Of all the ways of acquiring a mate in tribal India, mention the most frequent ways.

15. What is the relevance of the concept of household?

16. Is there empirical evidence to the prevalence of joint family in traditional India?

CHAPTER THIRTEEN

Marital Residence and Kinship

1. Marital residence

The residence rule is about where a couple stays after their marriage. **Patrilocal residence**refers to a pattern of residence in which a married couple lives with or near the husband's parents. **Matrilocal residence**refers to a pattern of residence in which a married couple lives with or near the wife's parents.

Of the 565 societies in Murdock's World Ethnographic Sample, 67% follow patrilocality, 15% are matrilocal, 7% bilocal, 4% avunculocal, and 5% neolocal.

Why should the majority of the societies follow patrilocality? It is because of patriarchy. Patriarchy is a universal phenomenon, therefore the domestic life in most societies is structured on patrilocality. Patrilocality leads to patrilineality. Patrilineality deals with the descent rule.

Rules of descentare the rules that connect individuals with particular sets of kin because of known or presumed common ancestry. **Patrilineal descent**refers to the rule of descent that affiliates individuals with kin of both sexes related to them through men only. **Matrilineal descent**refers to the rule of descent that affiliates individuals with kin of both sexes related to them through women only.

Matrilocality may lead to matrilineality. What factors may reduce patriarchy and contribute to matrilocality? Woman's contribution to work plays an important role. When the woman is contributing more, patriarchy cannot remain so strong. In a horticultural society, women may stay at a place and they may want their husbands to join them. What will this lead to? Matrilocality. And when a husband joins the wife's group, he will be called somebody's son or somebody's husband. A group develops over the woman's name. That is how matrilineality comes to be. Matrilocality over generations becomes matrilineality and patrilocality over generations becomes patrilineality.

If it is not about the entire society and only one or two individuals move to stay with their wives, it will be taken as an exception. But if a sufficient number of individuals are staying with their wives, then matrilineal systems may develop over a period of time.

A woman's contribution to the economy is the key factor. Still, the universal tendency of patriarchy is so strong that there is something more needed to explain matrilineality. First we have to understand that matrilineality is not a mirror image of patrilineality. Let's see how matrilineality works. Let's consider a scenario of two sisters and a brother in a horticultural society. After all the three marry, the husbands of the sisters come to stay with them while the brother moves out.

What happens here is that the brother continues to dominate the sisters. In a matriliny, the brother-sister relationship is important. The sister's child will be controlled not only by the father but also by the maternal uncle. How can a brother control the sister's children when he is not staying in the same house with his sister? He moves out after his marriage, but he will usually marry a woman from a house which is not far from his own house. Marriages in the matrilineal societies tend to be locally endogamous, meaning that the people tend to marry within a particular locality. The man does not go very far from his original house. That way he can be in touch with his sister's family though he lives at his wife's place.

A man has to take care of his sister's child, but at the same time, he has some responsibility towards his own son. So there could be some kind of conflict between one's own son and the sister's son. For a boy, it would be father vs uncle. For a woman, brother vs husband.

A patriarchal, patrilineal society avoids this conflict. The bride's side says to the groom's side, "We are giving our daughter to you, and hereafter she is your responsibility." A woman more or less surrenders to the house of her in-laws, and the husband assumes the centre stage. The in-laws become more important than the parents. The woman should adjust to the house to which she is sent. In patrilineal and patriarchal societies the rules of the game are very clear. The woman is subordinated to the man.

There is a very important factor that influences patriarchy: warfare. There are two kinds of warfare, internal and external. Internal means internal to the society, external means external to the society. Internal warfare can happen suddenly. External warfare, which is between one society and another society, can give more time to the people to prepare. Between matriliny and patriliny, which enables quick mobilisation of men? It is patriliny, for it is based on male consolidation. In matriliny, the position of the females is strong and the males are not connected well. Cross cultural evidence suggests that where most of the warfare is internal, the society is always patrilocal. But if the warfare that happens is usually only external, then the society may also be matrilocal.

Sometimes there is also another kind of residence rule, which is called avunculocal residence. When matrilocal societies are subjected to internal warfare, they may go for **avunculocal residence**, which is a pattern of residence in which a married couple settles with or near the husband's mother's brother. The boy is close to his uncle and so he takes his wife to his uncle's place instead of him going to his wife's place.

Neolocal residencerefers to a pattern of residence whereby a married couple lives separately, and usually at some distance, from the kin of both spouses. For the couple to lead an independent life, the economy should be commercial. Only then can they live on their own. Societies have generally been moving towards neolocality in our modern times.

Bilocal (or ambilocal) residencerefers to a pattern of residence in which a married couple lives with or near either the husband's parents or the wife's parents. They stay on the side where they have better opportunities or lesser risk. Studies show that recently depopulated societies tend to be bilocal – departing from their previously unilocal pattern. Depopulation may be caused by things such as new infectious diseases. Bilocality is also found among the foragers facing unpredictable resource crises.

2. Unilineal descent

Patrilineal descentrefers to the rule of descent that affiliates the individuals with the kin of both sexes related to them through the men only.

If a group is formed on the basis of patrilineal descent, every member of the group should trace their common ancestor through men only. If one can't do that, one is not a member of that kin group.

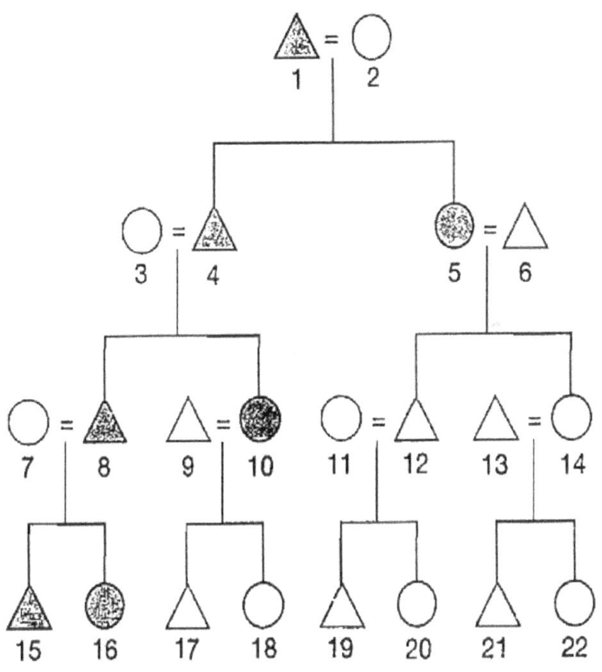

Fig.13.1: Patrilineal descent

(4) and (5) can say (1) is their father. (8) and (10) can say (1) is their grandfather. (15) and (16) can say (1) is their father's grandfather. Including (1), only 7 members belong to the patrilineal descent group. (12) has to say (1) is his mother's father, so (12) is not a member. (19) has to say (1) is his grandmother's father, so (19) is not a member.

Matrilineal descent refers to the rule of descent that affiliates individuals with the kin of both sexes related to them through women only. If the same society is arranged on the basis of matrilineal descent, how many people can trace themselves to (2) only through the women? (2) is the mother of (4) and (5), the grandmother of (12) and (14) and the mother's grandmother of (21) and (22). So a different set of 7 members belong to a kin group based on matrilineal descent.

Most societies are based on patrilineal descent and only some on matrilineal descent. As long as a society is following either matrilineal descent or patrilineal descent, it is said to be following **unilineal descent**, which means affiliation with a group of kin through descent links of one sex only.

Most societies have unilineal descent groups (UDGs). Individuals are automatically assigned to their kin groups and they don't get any choice. Instead, if the individuals can choose to join any group, then that society is said to be following **ambilineal descent**, which refers to the rule of descent that affiliates individuals with groups of kin related to them through men or women. In the diagram above, some can trace themselves to (1) through the father, or the mother's father, or the father's mother's father. Some can trace themselves to (2) as well.

3. Unilineal descent groups

Descent groups consist of people who trace their ancestry to a common ancestor. These groups can be lineages or clans. **Lineage** refers to a set of kin whose members trace descent from a common ancestor through known links. A **clan** refers toa set of kin whose members believe themselves to be descended from a common ancestor but can't specify the links back to that founder. A clan is often designated by a totem.

Lineages and clans are exogamous. Their members are regarded as siblings. Mate selection is influenced by clan membership. Lineages can be either matrilineage or patrilineage. Clans can be either patriclans or matriclans. Hindus call their clans gotras. Rules of exogamy contribute to alliances across the descent groups. These rules contribute to smooth relations across the kin groups in a society.

No society has just individuals and families, it also has groups. Groups in simple societies are kin-based. It is natural for a society to produce groups. If two brothers with their wives are left in a forest, they may evolve into two distinct groups over many generations – each group tracing its ancestry to a brother. Isn't groupism natural to humans? People differ in terms of things like what should be the basis of forming a group but groups have always been there.

A group is nothing but a collective identity – a common past, a common belief, an idea of a shared future. Simple societies have kin-based groups.Modern societies have non-kin based groups – state, nation, religion etc.

Groups are intermediaries between the individuals and the society, they serve certain purposes. Most simple societies have unilineal descent groups (UDGs), and only rarely they have ambilineal groups. Unilineal descent groups are more common because they offer clarity regarding membership.

UDGs perform certain economic functions. They may collectively own certain resources like land and forest. If a member faces an economic crisis, the other members will come to help him. Members support themselves on important occasions like births, initiations, marriages and funerals.

UDGs may perform political functions too. Clan leaders may be involved in settling disputes and maintaining order. Clans will be involved in the protection of the individuals against attacks from the members of other clans. Wars may be fought along clan lines.

UDGs have religious functions too. Clans have totems. Each clan may have separate religious functions associated with its totem.

Apart from lineages and clans, societies may also have phratries and moieties. **Phratry** refers to a unilineal descent group composed of a number of supposedly related clans. **Moiety** refers to a unilineal descent group in a society that is divided into two such maximal groups; there may be smaller unilineal descent groups as well.

The people in each moiety believe themselves to be descended from a common ancestor; they may not be able to specify how. Societies with moieties tend to be small. Aside from the fact that a society that has a phratry must have clans, all combinations of descent groups are possible.

There are some societies that have unilocal residence rather than UDGs. It means that related males or related females live together – without any strong sense of a group. What factors can push unilocality to give rise to UDGs? Warfare can be a factor, it tends to divide the society into distinct groups. UDGs therefore serve a very important political purpose.

4. *Social change*

A very important aspect of social change as societies evolved is the development of non-kin based groups. In a simple society, it is said that you are less than an insect if you don't have a kin, whereas kin is not that important for us in the modern society. Why is it so? Because we manage our needs through money. We buy things, we buy services – child care, hospital, education, etc. We get certain things as citizens, like protection through the police and the army.

In simple societies, there were no schools or colleges, no crèches, no old-age homes and no army. Kin groups fulfilled these functions. But as kin connection becomes less important, the size of an average kin group too is decreasing. Clans are losing importance; the family size is reducing. On the whole, the role of kin is on the decline.

Somebody might say, 'People nowadays don't bother about their brothers. People have become very selfish.' What does it mean? To what extent is it right? What does it say about our society? Often a person is regarded as selfish when he does not take care of a kin. But it is just the process of social change that the importance we attach to our kin has declined. Earlier, kin played a much more important role.

Is it true that man has become very selfish these days? Something like the rise in selfishness can be seen in terms of social change. We have reached a stage where you have to take care of yourself and you can buy many things from the society directly.

Earlier there was no buying. You had to be related to others. You had to be good to others, you had to be dependent. Now you only have to somehow earn money and with that money you can buy many things. So people have become more self-centred. That gives rise to this sense of selfishness. I am not using the word selfishness in a negative sense here, I am just stating it as a fact.

Let us look deeper into this. In a hunting-gathering society, there is a lot of sharing. Why do they share? Because there is no way of storing the food. Share what you have today, because you may not have any left tomorrow. So sharing was an adaptive trait then. But now there are ways of storing things, and ultimately we do it in the form of money. So acquisitiveness has become important.

Can you answer, 'Who are the good people between foragers and ourselves?' It is difficult to answer. But who are more selfish between foragers and ourselves? It is us. Selfishness need not be seen as a bad thing. It is just that our societies are organised on different lines. Do you see how changes in economy bring about changes in the value systems?

5. Bilateral kinship and double descent

Some societies do not have descent-based groups at all – be it patrilineal, matrilineal or ambilineal. These are societies with **bilateral kinship**, the type of kinship system in which individuals affiliate more or less equally with their mother's and father's relatives.The term **kindred**refers to a bilateral set of close relatives who may be called upon for some purpose. A kindred is not a definite group. It is an ego-centered group of kin. Aside from brothers and sisters, no two persons will have the same kindred group. When kinship matters, the kindred group would be larger, otherwise it would be smaller.

Double descent (double unilineal descent)is a system that affiliates individuals with a group of matrilineal kin for some purposes and with a group of patrilineal kin for other purposes. This is a combination of matrilineal descent and patrilineal descent.

This is not bilateral kinship where there are no descent-based groups at all.

Take a man's relationship with his grandparents. In bilateral kinship, all four grandparents are equal to him. In a unlineal descent, one grandparent is important; in a patrilineal descent, his paternal grandfather, in matrilineal descent, his material grandmother. In double descent, both the paternal grandfather and the maternal grandmother are important. This is not called bilineal descent to avoid confusion with bilateral kinship. It is also not called dual descent to avoid confusion with dual organisation.

The Ashanti have both matri-sibs and patri-sibs. Both of them are exogamous and totemic. Inheritance and succession to authority follow the female line and the avunculate exists but residence is patrilocal and the household consists of a patrilineal extended family. The matri-sibs are not localised but united by a common ancestor cult and special ceremonies. The Ashanti system is followed in other nearby tribes too.

Rivers (1906) described the Todas as organised into two endogamous moieties, each of which is divided into exogamous, non-totemic patri-sibs. The society is patrilineal and patrilocal. But Emeneau (1937) found that the Todas have double descent. He discovered the presence of matri-sibs among them. A moiety is now seen as intersecting matri-sibs and patri-sibs. This raises the possibility that many societies earlier described as unilineal could be double unilineal. At present time, the existence of double descent is found in widely scattered cultures across the world: West Africa, South Africa, India, Australia, Melanesia and Polynesia.

Except in rare cases, both patri-sibs and matri-sibs are exogamous. Inheritance and succession are usually patrilineal, except among the Ashanti. It has been suggested by some that double descent might result when exogamous matri-sibs come to adopt patrilocality and organise politically on a local basis.

6. Kinship terminology

The kinship terminology used in a society may reflect the prevailing kind of family in it, its rule of residence, its rule of descent and other aspects of social organisation. Kin terms may also give clues to the prior features of the society's social system, as these terms are very resistant to change. The major systems of kinship terminology are given below.

(1) Iroquois system

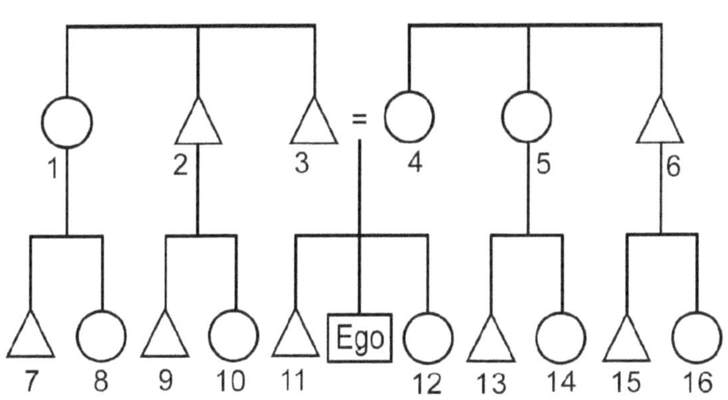

Fig. 13.2: Kinship terminology

This is exactly like South Indian system. The father and his brother get the same terms. (2,3) are the same. The mother and her sister get the same terms. (4,5) are the same. Parallel cousins are like one's own siblings. (9,11,13) and (10,12,14) are the same. Cross cousins are distinguished from parallel cousins. (7,15) and (8,16) get the same terms. (1) is one term and (6) another term. This terminology is essentially based on the parallel cousin vs cross cousin distinction. Parallel cousins are like one's one siblings and their parents are like one's own parents. So nuclear family terms are given to the families of parallel cousins. And cross cousins and their parents are clearly distinguished from the parallel cousins. Total kin terms are eight – four for the parental generation, four for one's own.

The terminology shows who can marry whom. This also shows patrilocality and patrilineality. Parallel cousins live in the same house, cross cousins in different houses.

(2) Inuit or Eskimo system

This is like an English family – who have terms only for the members of the nuclear family. All others are given only three terms – uncles, aunts and cousins. Total kin terms are seven: (3), (4), (11), (12), (1,5), (2,6), and (7,8,9,10, 13,14,15,16). This reflects a system where only nuclear family is important. There are no descent groups. This is a bilateral kinship that is ego-based.

(3) Sudanese system

The Sudanese system does not lump any of the relatives. The 16 people in the diagram have 16 kin terms. The terms are **descriptive**, meaning that a unique term is used for each relative. This is associated with political complexity, stratification and occupational specialisation.

(4) Hawaiian system

This system uses only four kin terms. People are classified only by the generation and the sex. No distinction is made between the nuclear family and what lies outside. The term for the father, his brother, and mother's brother is one and the same. The term for the mother, her sister, and the father's sister is the same. People of one's own generation are all brothers and sisters.

The kin terms for both the mother side and the father side are the same. This reflects an absence of unilineal descent groups. The societies are likely to have large extended families with bilocal residence patterns. The kin outside the nuclear family being given the same names means that many of these kin are considered important.

(5) Omaha and Crow systems

In the Iroquois system that we have seen earlier, there are eight different kin terms. Cross cousins are distinguished only by the gender. The Omaha system and the Crow system, however, deviate from the Iroquois in distinguishing whether a cross cousin is on the father side or the mother side. Also among the Omaha, the mother's brother and his son are given the same term. And among the Crow, the father's sister and her daughter are given the same term. Both Omaha and Crow have 9 kin terms. The Crow system is a mirror image of the Omaha system, except that the Omaha is based on patrilineal descent and the Crow on matrilineal.

Terms

1. Patrilocal residence: a pattern of residence in which a married couple lives with or near the husband's parents.

2. Matrilocal residence: a pattern of residence in which a married couple lives with or near the wife's parents.

3. Neolocal residence: a pattern of residence whereby a married couple lives separately, and usually at some distance, from the kin of both spouses.

4. Bilocal (or ambilocal) residence: a pattern of residence in which a married couple lives with or near either the husband's parents or the wife's parents.

5. Avunculocal residence: a pattern of residence in which a married couple settles with or near the husband's mother's brother.

6. Unilocal residence: a pattern of residence (patrilocal, matrilocal or avunculocal) that specifies just one set of relatives that the married couple lives with or near.

7. Rules of descent: rules that connect individuals with particular sets of kin because of known or presumed common ancestry.

8. Patrilineal descent: the rule of descent that affiliates individuals with kin of both sexes related to them through men only.

9. Matrilineal descent: the rule of descent that affiliates individuals with kin of both sexes related to them through women only.

10. Unilineal descent: affiliation with a group of kin through descent links of one sex only.

11. Ambilineal descent: the rule of descent that affiliates individuals with groups of kin related to them through men or women.

12. Lineage: a set of kin whose members trace descent from a common ancestor through known links.

13. Clan (sib):a set of kin whose members believe themselves to be descended from a common ancestor or ancestress but can't specify the links back to that founder. This is often designated by a totem.

14. Totem:a plant or animal associated with a clan as a means of group identification; may have other special significance for the group.

15. Phratry:a unilineal descent group composed of a number of supposedly related clans.

16. Moiety:a unilineal descent group in a society that is divided into two such maximal groups; there may be smaller unilineal descent groups as well.

17. Bilateral kinship: the type of kinship system in which individuals affiliate more or less equally with their mother's and father's relatives.

18. Kindred: a bilateral set of close relatives who may be called upon for some purpose.

19. Egois the reference point or focal person in the reckoning of kinship.

20. Double descent (double unilineal descent): a system that affiliates individuals with a group of matrilineal kin for some purposes and with a group of patrilineal kin for other purposes.

21. Classificatory terms: kinship terms that merge or equate relatives who are genealogically distinct from one another; the same term is used for a number of different kin.

22. Descriptive term: a unique term used for a distinct relative.

23. Consanguineal kin: one's biological relatives; relatives by birth.

24. Affinal kin: one's relatives by marriage.

25. Uxorilocal residence: equivalent to matrilocal, but specialised to instances where the wife's matri-kin are not aggregated in matrilocal and matrilineal kin groups.

26. Virilocal residence: equivalent to patrilocal, but specialised to instances where the husband's patri-kin are not aggregated in patrilocal and patrilineal kin groups.

Think on it

1. What is meant by a residence rule?

2. What is the difference between patrilocality and patriarchy?

3. What is the difference between matrilocality and matrilineality?

4. Why is patrilocality more common?

5. What circumstances give rise to matrilineality?

6. Why do matrilocal societies tend to follow local endogamy?

7. Explain avunculocal residence.

8. Explain how type of warfare affects residence rule.

9. What is the difference between neolocal residence and bilocal residence?

10. What is the difference between residence rule and descent rule?

11. What are unilineal descent groups?

12. What is an ambilineal descent?

13. What is the difference between lineage and clan?

14. Why do simple societies require unilineal descent groups?

15. What is a phratry? What is a moiety?

16. Why is there reduced importance to kinship in any advanced society?

17. How is bilateral kinship different from double descent?

18. Do Todas have double descent? Explain.

19. What do you know about the Iroquois kinship terminology?

20. How many kin terms does the Eskimo kinship terminology have?

21. How is the Omaha kinship terminology different from that of the Crow?

22. Which kinship system has the maximum number of kin terms? Which has the minimum?

CHAPTER FOURTEEN

Kinship Map of India

We are going to discuss the kinship systems in India, based on the work of Irawati Karve. She gave a comprehensive picture of kinships in India – from the north to the south and in the east. She found interesting patterns in these kinships. Kinship is a very important part of the culture and if people have the same culture, they may be sharing the same type of kinship system.

Karve divided India into several linguistic zones. These linguistic zones are nothing but cultural zones. If two languages are closely related to each other, the cultural practices of the people speaking those languages may also be closely related. If two languages are very distant and unconnected, maybe the cultures of the people speaking those languages are also much different. Cultural zones are therefore language zones. Karve found a pattern in how kinships change from the north to the south and what happens in the middle – the transition zone. She also observed the kinship systems in the east.

The basic type of kinship she describes is patrilocal and patriarchal – the variation being only in the extent of patriarchy. She explains how patriarchy is maintained across India.

1. How patriarchy operates

Kinships in a country like India may look like a labyrinthine network, but they are based on certain simple principles. If you understand the essentials, you understand many things. In a strong patriarchal system, will something like a sister-exchange be regarded desirable? In a sister-exchange, a man marries the sister of his brother-in-law. In such an arrangement, the man dominating the woman is very risky. In fact, he may not be dominating her, it may simply be her perception that she is being dominated – if she doesn't like her husband, she has only to complain to her brother and the payment will be made in kind. Sister-exchange therefore reduces male domination. This principle can be extended to many situations. If a group wants to dominate the women, that group should not give their women to a group from which it takes the women.

If you want to follow a system where you would be completely free in how you treat your wife or how you treat your daughter in law, from whom would you bring the women – from close relatives or distant? From distant relatives, because that enables control. For greater control of the women, should you bring them from a nearby place or from a far-off place? From a far-off place, because they may not be very familiar with their new place. Familiarity is power, so bring somebody from a far-off place.

In such situations where domination of women happens, what will be the hierarchical relationship between the group that is taking the brides and the group that is giving the brides? Who will feel inferior? It's the group that gives the brides.

Why is this inequality between the bride's group and the groom's group? Why is the bride's family so vulnerable? Patrilocality plays a very powerful role here. The bride is going to be with the groom's family for the rest of her life. Why do the bride's parents, along with the bride, cry in the parting ceremony when they are sending off their daughter? Is it simply for ritualistic reasons? Notwithstanding the plans the bride's parents might have made for her before the marriage, they can never be certain about their daughter's life after the marriage. Till not long ago – and even now to some extent – they helplessly depended on the groom's family. They don't know how their daughter is going to be treated at her new home. She may be treated well or she may be not. If she is not treated well, the solution would not be obvious. People can't go for breakups just like that. A breakup is a very costly affair, in every way. The daughter-in-law of a family is generally in a vulnerable position. The groom's parents may say, 'We will not treat her like our daughter-in-law, we will treat her like our own daughter!' But that cannot be easily believed. So there is a risk, there is an uncertainty. That is why the parting ceremony after the marriage is a moment of deep emotions.

The bride's parents could say 'If there is a problem for you at your in-law's house, don't tell us'. Why? They are sending a message, 'Try to resolve the issues by yourself'. A woman is not supposed to carry tales against her in-laws to her parents. Mostly because the parents can't do anything about the situation even if they know about it. And if they try to do something, it may worsen it. Basically, the understanding is that 'We try to be careful before giving daughter, but once given, we can only wish her good luck'.

Patrilocality is a very powerful thing. A woman is going to a stranger's house, they are a group – the brothers and their parents. The groom's group may think, 'This woman may disrupt our family. She may want to take her husband out of here'. That family is based on the consolidation of the brothers. They and their parents – it is one unit. The brothers may also have been married. They may have wives coming from different places. This system is based on male consolidation and the women come into the family as strangers.

That is the reason why a daughter-in-law has no power at all. When they are looking out for a suitable daughter-in-law, the group will consider, 'What kind of a woman are we bringing? Will she respect our whole family and not just her husband?'. They try to see if this new woman would fit in their family, with all the brothers, their parents, and their wives.

The groom's family will think of how this new woman will be able to connect with them, whereas the bride's family has a concern as to how she will be treated there. Both the families may be taking the risk, but the risk that the bride's parents are taking is much more, because the power is on the groom's side. It is after all the groom's house, his place and who is supposed to adjust? It's the bride.

How does this adjustment take place? Usually the people who get married are from the same cultural tradition. Both the families have an idea as to how a wife should behave and how a husband should behave. In the olden times, the groom and the bride were not even supposed to see each other before the marriage, only the families would meet. The boy and the girl were just supposed to nod, the parents were supposed to take care of who is good for their son or daughter.

These old ways of marriage are changing. Previously, it was more of a relationship between groups. A girl is entering another group, that girl is a wife to somebody but she is other things to other people. She is a daughter-in-law, she is a sister-in-law, she is an aunt. She is expected to play many roles. She cannot say, 'I will take care only of my husband and my children'. She is expected to take care of her husband's brother's children too, in some way. She may be sharing work with others. One daughter-in-law may regularly go to the fields, and another daughter-in-law may stay at home, taking care of all the children. Marriage was not just a relationship between one man and one woman, like it is viewed in the modern times.

In fact, if you are familiar with a joint family, you are not likely to see a husband and a wife being together on their own. The brothers would be at one place, and the women would be at another place. The husband and wife sitting together in some kind of personal space is not seen generally and is also not appreciated. In such a large joint family, the children may be closer to a woman other than their own mother. The emphasis is not on a woman's personal relationship with her husband or her even personal relationship with her own children.

If you have a daughter, you could be controlled by her in-laws. Not only would you be controlled, but the daughter is also not of any use to you after the marriage. She is taking a large amount of dowry money with her and going away. She would not be there to take care of her parents. Under such conditions, could the parents normally prefer to have a daughter? That is why a daughter used to be seen as a liability and a son used to be seen as an asset. When your child will not be useful to you after getting married, even when you yourself would be in a vulnerable position in your old age, then why would you want to have a daughter?

Let's see if this aspect has changed at least now. Nowadays, a woman may want to work or a man may want his wife to work. It means more income. But is there any change in the thinking about who should take care of the woman's parents? The parents may not want to stay with their son-in-law, and the in-laws too may not agree for it.

That is how it is with a joint family. And a good deal of it continues into the modern times. The situation being such, it is easy to see why it could be a disaster to the family if a boy falls in love with a girl. That girl may say, 'I love you' but it means 'only you,' and she may want nothing to do with his family. Such a thing is good as long as both are in a park but the home is not a park.

Love is seen as a very unfavourable thing. It could be considered a disaster to the family. Because when we are talking about love, we are talking about love between individuals. But the family is not about an individual. That is why love is never encouraged. Marriage was a group arrangement. An advantage to the individuals in this group arrangement was that their responsibility towards their upkeep was shared. The boy just had to play his particular role and the girl had to play her particular role, and if there was a problem they faced, then the others would get involved too. If the groom's family has any serious problems from the girl, they will go and talk to her parents. Conflict is managed through group effort. On the contrary, if the boy and the girl marry of their own choice, and if there arises a conflict between them, who would have to manage it? It is too personal and bears an uncertain outcome, there is no system to deal with it.

In a modern marriage, who should listen to whom? That is not settled. The boy has certain habits and the girl has certain habits, and if they are not compatible, who should change for whom? Both of them may keep arguing. Traditionally it was very clear. It was the girl who had to change and adjust her ways always. In the modern times, the individuals are asked to choose their life partners and they are also asked to face any problems that may arise by themselves in their individual capacity.

Ironically, marriages now are more likely to fail not because they have become less important, but because they have become more important. The relationship between a man and a woman is becoming so much more important in a nuclear family as compared to that in a joint family. In a nuclear family, if a woman is not so efficient at domestic work, then that family will be affected. In a joint family, however, a woman who is not good at child care can do other things. The same thing applies to man's earning. In a nuclear family, if a man can't earn, the family will get affected but in a joint family not all the brothers need to earn. One brother may be earning more than all the others, some brothers may have regular jobs and some may not. And one brother may be meant exclusively for running errands, he does not have to earn, and yet he plays an important role in the family in his own way. One brother may be managing the family income, another may focus on taking care of the children's needs. One brother may specialize in relationships and kin connections. The point is that there is less dependence on the dynamics between a husband and wife in the joint family. Sociologist Talcott Parsons says: marriage in a nuclear family is like an overloaded circuit, the fuse of which can get burnt anytime.

Patriarchy works in favour of those who have sons. Those who have daughters are at a loss. To the question as to why woman's side follows patriarchal system, the answer is that they follow because they can't stop it and so they think they should have sons. They should at least have one son for their old age security. When a couple has only daughters, usually they would go for more and more children expecting a son. They may only end up having many more daughters. And it is this context that sometimes led to the practice of foeticide or infanticide because a couple might be desperately trying to get a male child. This was how an uneven sex ratio emerged in the Indian society.

2. North Indian system

Let us now look at the specific rules that govern the kinship systems in India. The North Indians follow a system that promotes maximum patriarchy and maximum domination. A bride is not taken from any of the nearby clans. This is called the four-clan or four-gotra rule: a boy should not marry from one's own clan, from the mother's clan, from the father's mother's clan, from the mother's mother's clan.

A woman moves from her group to live with another group, but she belongs to the clan into which she was born. When the above-mentioned four clans are eliminated as a potential group to get a girl from, then the girl is likely to come from a distant place. The four clans are ruled out, but the mate selection has to happen within the caste.

In the north, they also get a bride from a distant region. It is not simply excluding four clans but it should exclude some geographical region. It is locally exogamous.

Geographically, what unit can be considered as endogamous? Will anybody marry somebody from a group speaking a different language? Not likely. The language has to be the same, so a linguistic region is an endogamous unit. These are the various background criteria of selection of a bride in North India. Because one's own clan and the three specified clans that are close to it are eliminated, cross cousins and parallel cousins are excluded from any marriage considerations.

In North India, a woman as a daughter leads a relatively free life, but she will experience a very restricted existence as a daughter-in-law. The dress code of a daughter too can be very different from that of a daughter-in-law.

In a village, there would be many young women, some of them daughters and some of them daughters-in-law. Who will have more freedom? It is the daughters. Staying with the in-laws means leading a more disciplined life, but staying with the parents means being less constrained by such discipline. In a village, the daughters can be easily differentiated from the daughters-in-law. The daughters will have their own associations and the daughters-in-law will have their own.

Another rule in North India is that if village A is getting a large number of girls from village B, then village A will be considered superior to village B. The girls from A will not be given to B. Women flow in one direction only. The people have a saying there, 'Boy from the west, girl from the east'.

Unidirectional flow of woman facilitates better control of them. It sets up a hierarchy between the bride-givers and the bride-takers. To the extent that the women can flow in the opposite direction, you are losing the control of the women living with you. So the kinship systems can be examined in terms of the direction of the flow of women. If women can move geographically or kin-group-wise only in one direction, then it is an indication of a strong patriarchy. North India reinforces patriarchy.

In North India, one can see the hierarchy among the clans. The clans within a caste are given a hierarchical order. The bride-giving clans are regarded as inferior to the bride-taking clans. The man comes from a higher clan and the woman from a lower clan – this is called hypergamy. Hypogamy, where the girl is from a higher clan, is not allowed.

3. South Indian system

The South Indian kinship system is far less hierarchical than its northern counterpart. Marvin Harris explains in his Cultural Anthropology why there is a difference between North India and South India in kinship systems. He says that rice cultivation was important in South India, and in rice cultivation, transplantation is a very crucial step, done by women. When women play a key role at a crucial stage of the economic activity, then their power increases.

How does mate selection work here? Cross-cousin marriage is allowed. This in itself is enough to change the entire kinship system. What do matri-cross and patri-cross marriages do to the kinship system?

In a patrilateral cross-cousin marriage, the girl will go to her mother's brother's house. Will her father-in-law act like any other father-in-law now? No, he can't because his daughter-in-law is simply his sister's daughter. So she will be treated like his daughter, and the girl feels much more secure. She can be as free as at her own home, and her husband is only her cousin. He can't really behave like a domineering husband. They might have played together as children. This kind of marriage doesn't support a strong patriarchy.

And there is nothing like hierarchy between the boy's family and the girl's family. The family head's sister is in one family, and the girl from that family is now in this family. When the flow of women happens in both the directions, patriarchal hierarchy is not possible. There is more equality between the sexes. Not only that women move in both directions, but here they are also moving only to the places of their close kin.

Till recently, this cross-cousin marriage was the preferred system in South India. The situation was such that if a man is not marrying his cousin, there had to be a reason for it. The sister can ask her brother 'Why are you not taking my daughter?' The brother may say, 'Okay, there is some problem, so my son cannot marry your daughter, but I will help in getting her married'.

In a patrilateral cross-cousin marriage, the power equation is gone and there is more of intimacy between the husband and the wife. It is not that all families tend to go for a patri-cross marriage; still, even if a considerable number of families go for a patri-cross marriage, it changes the culture of how a woman should be treated and how a bride should be seen. When patrilateral cross cousins can be married, this in itself changes the rules. The woman will be free even after her marriage. This changes the patriarchal rules of what a daughter can be and what a daughter-in-law can be. The young women of a village are not divided into daughters and daughters-in-law.

Irawati Karve says that in the South Indian system, kin groups are consolidated through cross-cousin marriages. The South Indian kinship system contributes to the consolidation of existing kin links. It allows patrilateral cross-cousin marriages as well as matrilateral cross-cousin marriages. In contrast, the North Indian system expands the kin links by absorbing new groups.

One can also look at what is happening to the kin groups in terms of patriarchy. In North India, there is maximum patriarchy, in South India, it is minimum. Irawati Karve thinks that the North Indian system developed that way because there were pastoralists in North India. Pastoralists seek connections with people from distant regions, because they prefer to take their animals and move across a large geographical region, going by the availability of the fodder. In South India, there was no pastoralism.

4. Central Indian system

Now we will discuss the difference between a matrilateral cross-cousin marriage and a patrilateral cross-cousin marriage. In the north, no cross-cousin marriage is allowed. In the south, both matrilateral and patrilateral cross-cousin marriages are allowed and favoured. In the central region, only matrilateral cross-cousin marriage is allowed. Why should this be so?

There is in fact a big difference between matrilateral and patrilateral cross-cousin marriages. They are not mirror images of each other because in both of these cross-cousin marriages, the system is patrilocal and patrilineal. Let's work out what it means.

Patri cross cousins

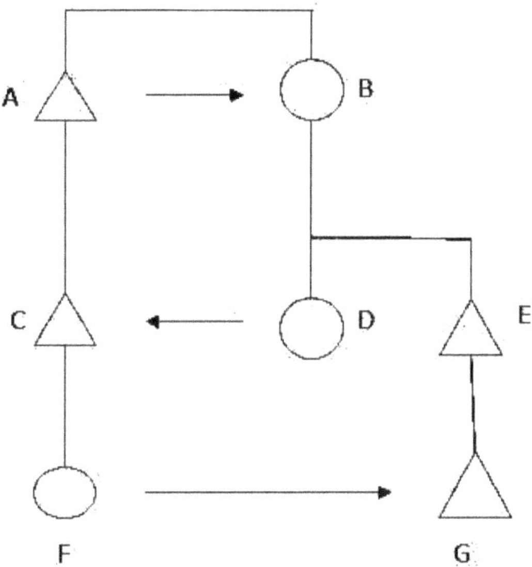

Fig 14.1: Patri-cross cousin marriage

Let us assume patrilateral cross-cousin marriages between two groups. C marrying D is patri-cross marriage. D is coming to the group from which B had left a generation ago. B and D moved in opposite directions. There is bidirectional flow of women. In the next generation, when G marries F, F moves opposite to the movement of D. There is exchange of women in both the directions between the two groups. When the flow of women is bidirectional, a hierarchy does not develop between the groups.

When C is marrying D, it is a matri-cross marriage. D moved in the same direction that A moved a generation ago. When F marries G, G is also moving in the same direction as A and D did before. This means that matricross cousin marriages involve only unidirectional flow of women. Group hierarchy can be maintained that way. The bride-taking group is superior to the bride-giving group.

Matri cross cousins

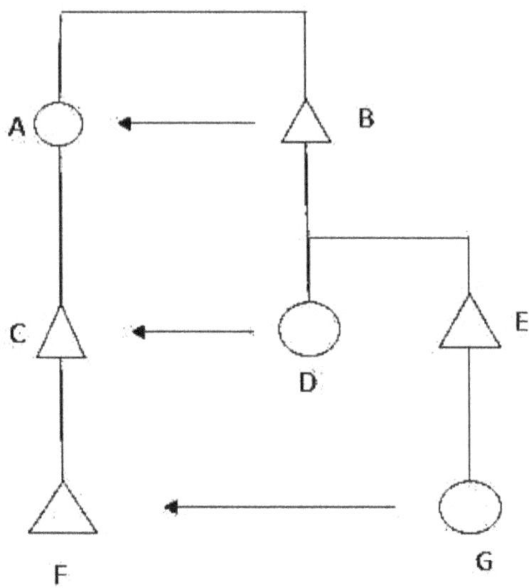

Fig 14.2: Matri-cross cousin marriage

North India, where no cross-cousin marriage is allowed, is more hierarchical than Central India. Central India, where only matrilateral cross-cousin marriage is allowed is more hierarchical than South India. South India which allows both matrilateral and patrilateral cross-cousin marriages is the least hierarchical. Irawati Karve found these patterns in what she called the kinship map of India. On the eastern side, the kinship systems are different. They are different cultural and linguistic groups.

The three siblings of my mother married their cross-cousins who are siblings themselves. This is an example of how closely knit South Indian families can get. In the diagram below, (1) is my mother.

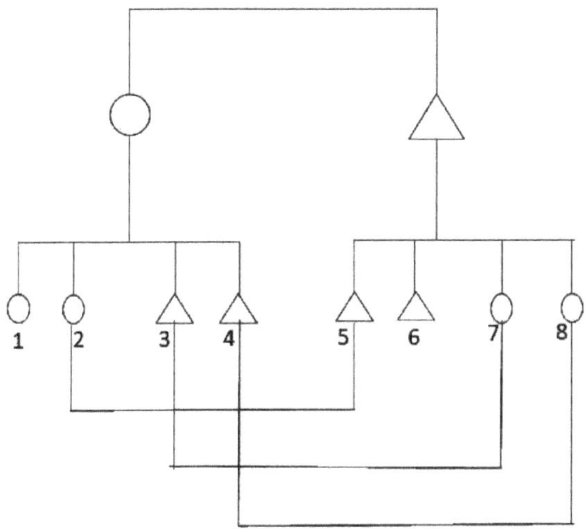

Fig. 14.3: Close-knit families

Think on it

1. How is a linguistic zone related to a kinship system?

2. How is patrilocality an important aspect of patriarchy?

3. How is marriage in a nuclear family different from that in a joint family?

4. Explain how uneven sex ratio is a result of the kinship system?

5. What is the four-clan rule? How does it strengthen patriarchy?

6. What is meant by 'Boy from the west and girl from the east.'?

7. How does local exogamy reinforce patriarchy?

8. Why is clan-wise hypogamy not acceptable in North India?

9. Are both patrilateral and matrilateral cross-cousin marriages allowed in South India?

10. How does a cross-cousin marriage weaken patriarchy?

11. How did pastoralism shape the North Indian kinship system?

12. Which cross-cousin marriage is allowed in parts of central India? Explain.

CHAPTER FIFTEEN

Changes in Family Structure

We are going to discuss contemporary trends with respect to the institution of family. We will start from our understanding of simple societies. In matters of relationships, the basic difference between simple and complex societies, as we have seen already, is the declining importance of kinship.

In simple societies, the kin group is very important. Kin groups are useful in the context of marriages and serve economic, political, and religious purposes. Kin groups offer protection. They fight wars together. They are like insurance for an individual. Because there is no grouping other than kin-based groups, kinship is everything in simple societies. In a complex society, something called structural differentiation happens, to use the term coined by Talcott Parsons. Modern societies have different structures performing different functions, there are structures of child care, structures of religion, structures of war, and political and economic structures. More structures keep emerging and they all have specialised functions. The world is moving towards more specialisation.

Correspondingly, the typical size of the kin group has reduced. The size of an average family also has reduced. Extended families are dwindling, being divided into nuclear families. **Extended family** refers to a family consisting of two or more single-parent, monogamous, polygynous or polyandrous families linked by a blood tie. **Nuclear family** refers to a family consisting of a married couple and their children.

In India, a joint family is a type of extended family. It is a family unit where the brothers, their wives and children live together with their parents and only those sisters who are unmarried. The Indian joint family is based on the consolidation of sons. Daughters move to their husbands' families after marriage.

Extended families are becoming nuclear all over the world. What is the basic reason for it? Prior to the Industrial Revolution in the 19[th]century, most people depended only on agriculture for their livelihoods. Brothers would work together. But industrialisation required skills and education, and brothers would get different opportunities. Their education levels were different, their incomes were different. People moved to towns. Industrialisation led to rapid urbanisation. The traditional model of all the sons of a family working together was not viable anymore. This was a paradigm shift that happened when the focus of the economy moved from agriculture to industry. It was also a change from feudalism to capitalism. Feudalism was an agriculture-based model, capitalism was industry-based.

A nuclear family carries out all the functions of a family: sex, reproduction, socialisation of children and sexual division of labour. In a traditional nuclear family the man was the bread winner and woman was the housekeeper. Minimal unit of a family which carries out all the functions of a family is a nuclear family. For the better part of the day, the man would be out and work. The man was supposed to face the world in the struggle of survival, the woman was expected to be his support, the source of love and affection in the family. When the man was in stress, the woman was his comfort. Because of the woman, the man became much more capable and the industry would get much more out of him. Because the man was being supported by a network at home, the capitalism could draw much more out of him. Industrialisation thus brought about a significant level of nuclearisation of family.

Some sociologists, like Talcott Parsons, thought that once the family is nuclear, then its form would final and right. Parsons thought that families will turn nuclear and stay there. However, what happened was somewhat different. Change came from other sources such as feminism. Though women worked in factories right from the beginning of the Industrial Revolution, a greater number of them joined the work force during World War I. After the War, they did not like being confined to home once again. A large number of women experienced the freedom of going out. By that time, universal education spread in the Western world and the general education levels were increasing. Many started questioning why only the man should be a family's breadwinner, with the woman being confined to the home. Why can't the woman also work and contribute to the economy when she is perfectly capable of doing it? The traditional role of the woman in a family could not be taken for granted anymore.

Traditionally, man had been dominating woman. The man was supposed to go out and earn and the woman was supposed to be at home and take care of the children. This was the gender-based division of work. In this model, the man was supposed to be more educated than the woman and also older than her. Why was the man supposed to be older? Because he was supposed to be more knowledgeable. He was supposed to provide leadership. Man with an earning ability, higher qualification and age – it facilitated patriarchy. But all this began to be questioned. Feminists questioned the traditional division of labour and said that women also can go out and earn. They demanded equal opportunities in education and jobs.

Feminism could be possible because many countries of the world became democratic by the middle of the twentieth century. Democracy means equality. The equality is not only among men but also between man and woman. Democracy is a strong ideology. Such ideological changes happened because of modernisation. Modernisation values freedom, or liberty. It also values equality. Earlier, these values were not there. In a traditional Hindu society, equality was not a value. Loyalty was a value. Freedom was not a value, obedience was a value. 'Obey the elders, follow the traditions'. Those were the old values, and all that was changing.

Industrialisation brought about economic opportunities. Modernisation brought about new values. They could happen because of technological changes. Industrialisation is a dramatic change of the level of technology in a society.

Technology also gave man and woman a great control over the reproductive process. Because of the pill, sex was no more linked to reproduction. One could have sex without having children. Family planning became possible. Women became free from the burden of unwanted pregnancies. Lack of control over reproduction and having to give birth to many children was the main thing that had tied down women for thousands of years. This major constraint began to disappear.

Extended families changed to nuclear families, and then a great change happened within the nuclear family itself. The main change was in the division of labour. The contribution of the woman increased, she gained more rights. Patriarchy started crumbling.

Beyond nuclear family

What are the more recent trends in the family structure? The nuclear family itself has come under stress. New attitudes and values have come up – marriage for intimacy, marriage for love, and not for any economic reasons. A man and woman can decide what they want from their marriage – they don't have to follow any traditional roles. Individual freedom has become a chief value.

Marriage has become individualised. While this may be good in some ways, it is also contributing to marital instability. Divorce rates are shooting up. In many religions of the world, a marriage is considered a sacrament. In Hinduism, a marriage partnership is supposed to last for seven lives. Marriage is becoming more like a social contract with certain specific expectations by both the parties. And one of the expectations being love itself. And then when those expectations are not met, a separation becomes likely.

Because of these trends, even certain divorce laws are also changing. Earlier, the husband or the wife had to prove how the other person was wrong or unsuitable in order to get a divorce. There had to be causes such as adultery, domestic violence, or infertility. But now no-fault divorces are in vogue. The husband and the wife just have to say in the court, 'We don't want to live together'. This is divorce by mutual consent. In India, a couple can separate anytime between six months to one year after filing the petition for divorce. With the rise of no-fault divorces, the stigma associated with a divorce is being reduced.

Is the institution of marriage being rejected? It appears like people are not really rejecting the idea of marriage as such, because people who get divorced usually go on to get married again. Remarriage rates have been increasing. The number of marriages per population is increasing. People have not given up on marriage. They usually think that their particular choice was wrong, so they might want to experiment with some other person. Between men and women, it has been found that men are more likely to remarry, compared to women.

This situation is leading to a variety of family structures. Single parent families are becoming not uncommon. There could be occasions where a man comes up with his children and a woman comes up with hers and they marry. These are called reconstituted families or blended families.

Men and women are doing a lot of experimentation. Marriage is becoming more like a negotiation: 'This is what I expect from you in return for which this is what you get from me'. The roles are not defined clearly by default. Partners negotiate in this process, whether explicitly or through implicit understanding. Particularly in reconstituted families, the roles are vague. What is the role of a step mother? What is the role of a step father? What are their rights? We see a lot of innovation going on. But what is the most important thing that is happening behind all these changes in the nature and structure of family? If you have to identify one thing that is underlying all these changes, what would it be? All the changes in the nature of family and kinship are changes that are increasing woman's power. Why should the status of woman be linked to divorce rates? It's because women are refusing to play the old roles given to them in a patriarchal society.

For a woman, marriage is no longer meant for economic support, as it used to be the case earlier. She is in a position to take care of herself financially. So the original reason for entering the institution of marriage itself is being undermined.

How do you explain the increase in the divorce rates? It is the change in the woman – in her role and her expectations. Not always but often enough the phenomenon of a changing woman and an unchanging man can explain the marital crisis. Man is being threatened by the rise of woman. Earlier, the man could control and dominate the woman, but now he is not able to do so, and he is also not being able to rise to meet the new demands of love!

People are also pursuing alternatives to the traditional notion of marriage. Live-in relationship is one such. Same-sex marriages are also on the rise, with many countries giving them a legal status. How can same-sex couples get children? They can, through adoption or with the help of donors. So same-sex marriages and staying single with an adopted child or a child conceived with the help of donor are the emerging trends. Divorced individuals could also choose to remain single, with or without their children. And finally, staying single all one's life with no marriage and no children is also an option that many men and women are going for.

What can we make of all these things? What is it that men and women are generally seeking? Is a man seeking freedom from responsibilities or is it freedom from narrow framework of tradition? A woman adopting a child and not marrying anybody – what is she trying? Freedom from responsibility or freedom from the oppression of tradition? It is freedom from the tradition. The woman is showing the courage to live with an experimental attitude rather than blindly following old customs.

Being in a live-in relationship, with or without an intention to get married at some point – what is it that the man and the woman are seeking? They are seeking freedom. They don't want to follow the tradition that has come down to them from one generation to another. Whether it be freedom from the tradition or whether it be freedom from risk and responsibility, they are seeking some kind of freedom. Without intending it, these people are shaping the culture. They are questioning the approach to life followed by their parents and grandparents, they are boldly trying to choose their own lifestyles, with a clarity of mind. It means negotiation with the culture itself. It is not 'how should I be a good husband or a good wife?' People are finding out what is to be good? It is boldness. Is it not?

Terms

1. Extended family: a family consisting of two or more single-parent, monogamous, polygynous or polyandrous families linked by a blood tie.

2. Nuclear family:a family consisting of a married couple and their children.

3. Family:a social and economic unit consisting minimally of a parent and a child.

Think on it

1. Is the size of kin group reducing due to modernisation? Explain.

2. What is meant by structural differentiation?

3. What is the difference between extended family and Hindu joint family?

4. How did industrialisation change family?

5. How did feminism change family?

6. How did reproductive technology change family?

7. What are the changes taking place within a nuclear family?

8. How do you explain increase in divorce rates?

9. What is a blended family?

10. What are the alternatives to traditional marriage? Why are they being pursued?

Movie Review: Ninnu Kori

Most Indian films are based on the premise that if you love someone, you can't love anyone else, meaning that if you get romantically involved with one more person, your original love is not true. The 2017 Telugu movie Ninnu Kori, directed by Shiva Nirvana argues differently.

Uma Maheshwara Rao (Nani) and Pallavi (Nivetha Thomas) are youngsters who have fallen in love. It is just a regular kind of love that takes place with Vizag city as the background. But Pallavi knows her parents would never agree to their marriage and so she proposes that they should elope. Uma however refuses to do so, asking Pallavi instead to wait till he is in a position to be able to take care of her. He then goes to Delhi to do his Ph.D. Meanwhile, Pallavi is in a serious quandary, her father has brought an alliance, insisting on marriage, and she doesn't know what to do. Seeing that Uma is very much involved with his research, and deciding not to disrupt his education, she accepts her father's choice, gets married to Arun (Aadhi Pinisetty).

Uma is devastated when he gets to know about the marriage. Slowly he turns into an alcoholic, neglecting his career. Years later, Uma is settled in the US with her husband, and incidentally Uma too goes to the US.

Both Uma and Pallavi had genuine concern for each other, their love was true. Each of them could have acted differently, taking a decisive step towards marriage. But despite all their fondness for each other and their dreams of living together, they have ended up in a situation where Uma is depressed and Pallavi is married to another person. From this point, the movie pursues its unique theme; it turns out that Pallavi is happily married.

Realizing to her great consternation that Uma is becoming self-destructive, Pallavi meets Uma and tells him that she is very happy in her marriage and he should move on and be happy. She says, "My husband loves me so much, it is he who told me that love does not begin with one person, nor does it end with one person." Uma does not understand it, he does not think it is possible. He tells her, "If you did not marry the one you loved, there is no way you can be happy in your marriage. It is impossible, you are deceiving yourself.' Pallavi wants to convince him that he is mistaken. She makes a simple proposal, she asks him to stay at her house for 10 days to see for himself if she is happy. At the end of it, if he believes that she is happy, he should move on with his life and quit his self-destructive ways. But if he finds on any reasonable basis that she is unhappy in any way, then she is willing to annul her marriage.

I expected the movie to go in the direction of Pallavi winning her case. If a character makes such a profound statement as love does not begin or end with one person, I thought the movie would go on to prove this rather radical thesis. But it was far less predictable than I thought.

Uma doesn't remain a passive observer, he tries in any way he can to expose what he thinks is the reality of their marriage. He lets Arun know about his days of romance with Pallavi in Vizag, he tries to create a rift between the couple who struggle to keep things intact.

The twist comes when Pallavi finds out that Arun is having an affair. She can hardly believe it, she is in shock. She invited Uma to show him how great her marriage was, but things turned out to be this way. To the further surprise of the viewers, Uma who has been making attempts to break Pallavi's marriage is just as shocked, rather than delighting in this turn of events. He cannot stomach that his beloved is being cheated by her husband.

Uma's true love for Pallavi comes out when he becomes sad for her, even though it could mean that she will now be his. Wishing the girl's happiness and well-being even when it means losing her – is the mark of true love.

Happily though, it now turns out that Arun was not in fact having any affair, it was just a misunderstanding. Uma bridges the gap between the couple and goes on his way. He starts looking out for girls in a matrimonial site, hoping to find the right person. His intention now is to marry first and then find love within the marriage.

CHAPTER SIXTEEN

Feminism

1) Schools of feminism

We can say that any school of thought that is trying to empower woman or free woman from the domination of man is feminism. But If any ideology says in any way that man has the right to dominate women, then it cannot be feminism. **Cultural feminism**says that man and woman are different and play different roles. They are born different, their roles are different but equally important. They should be socialised to better fulfil their roles, a boy to become a man, a girl to become a woman.

How is a woman different from a man? Woman has strong qualities of care and affection. Man is more aggressive. They are born with different tendencies. Socialisation can work on those differences, and they will become more different from each other. This does not mean domination by man. This is not taking a position that woman should not go to work. We should design a society on the basis of inherent differences between man and woman but free from gender domination.

Cultural feminism says: do not take male activity as the reference for woman, let woman find out her own activity. Just as man is not considered inferior because he cannot give birth to children, women too should not be judged on the basis of men's capabilities. That is the position of cultural feminists.

Liberal feminismsays there are inequalities between the sexes in our society. We should strive to remove those inequalities. We must try to achieve equality. This should be done through providing better education and job opportunities to women, through politics, economy, and law and also by reorganising work within the family.

The liberal feminists criticise the traditional division of work within the family in patriarchal societies. Liberal feminists would disagree with cultural feminists in many things. Inequalities in power and access to resources is unfair to women. The society should be changed. Women should have equal access to resources, to positions in politics and administration. This also means that home should be changed; you cannot have the old division of labour at home and still be able to create job opportunities for women. There should be change within home itself, to begin with. This is liberal feminism.

Another school of thought is **radicalfeminism,**which says that patriarchy is the very centre of all problems. It is from patriarchy that all the other problems are coming. All other problems include economic problems, political problems, issues at home, and everything. Man creates economic structures, political structures, education, fashion, everything in a way that reinforces patriarchy.

It is not that together man and woman should create a just society but it is that woman should hold that man's attitude should be regarded the most serious problem.

Patriarchy is the enemy. Patriarchy is not one of the problems to a radical feminist. It is the fundamental problem, everything else is secondary. Everything that you see in the modern society has something to do with patriarchy. It is because of patriarchy that this whole system we live in came to be like this. So abolish patriarchy, put an end to it. Women should collectively work, actively seeking to overthrow patriarchy.

There is another school called **structural feminism,**which says that you have to look at the position of woman as a relationship between various groups in terms of class, caste, and community. Woman suffers as a result of the conflict between various groups, in class conflicts, in religious conflicts, etc. Women's problems are a problem of social structure.

Structural feminism says that woman suffers because of the way the social structure is. A Dalit woman suffers because of the lower caste, a poor woman suffers because of the lower class. Muslim women in India suffer during Hindu-Muslim clashes. Structural issues in a society affect women much more than men.

There is also **postmodern feminism,**which asks basic questions on what it is to be a woman in the first place. More basic questions are asked on what actually gender is.

Some of the issues raised under feminism by some feminists may be relevant to some women and may not be relevant to others. The issues that are highlighted and the solutions that are proposed have to be critically examined. The issue of the right to dress the way one wants, for example, may be relevant to some classes of women and not to the women of other classes.

2) *Waves of feminism*

In the US, the first wave of feminism surged when voting rights were given to the women in the 1920s. In 1960s and 70s, there was the second wave of feminism, which was concerned about many economic and political issues and those related to family, patriarchy, and gender division of labour. They said a woman has to be treated as an independent person with economic and political rights, not simply as a member of family.

The feminist movement in the 60s was started by Betty Friedan, a writer. She was a good mother and a good wife, but felt a sense of meaningless in life. She called it a problem which has no name, and she found that many of her friends also felt that way. Is a woman meant to be just a wife and a mother? Does she not she have a bigger role in life and society? The right to vote is fine, but what else? Is a woman's life simply meant to stay at home and take care of the family?

The third wave of feminism started in the 1990s. There was the collapse of the USSR, there were new trends of globalisation and neo-liberalism. In the more recent years, the rise of the Internet and social media favoured women's liberation.

In the case of India, the socio-religious reform movements of the 19[th]century and the freedom struggle in the first half of the 20[th]century constituted the first wave of women's liberation. During the socio-religious reform movements, many efforts were made to raise the woman's social status. Many women-related reforms happened. During the freedom struggle, the women took part in mass protests on a large scale.

In 1950, our Constitution came into effect and it was women-friendly. Indian women got voting rights just about 30 years after American women got it. This could happen because our Constitution was radical and made use of the progress that happened in the Western countries.

The West influenced the socio-religious reform movements of the 19[th]century.The West inspired our own freedom struggle. The West influenced the framing of our Constitution too. The movement of feminism is a part of a long process of modernisation.

What is modernisation about? It is about liberty and equality. Feminism is nothing but the concepts of liberty and equality applied to women, and to the context of man-woman relationships. This did not happen for a long time after the concepts of liberty and equality became part of collective awareness. The American Revolution declared that all men are created equal – but sadly it turned out that men here meant only men and did not include women. It also turned out that it did not include slaves. What was the English Revolution about? It was about the King versus the Parliament, the rulers versus the people. But there was no focus on the inequalities among the people. But by the time Indian Constitution was drafted, many developments took place on the path of modernisation. Our Constitution gave all adults voting rights – regardless of religion, caste, class, and gender.

The second wave of Indian feminism started in the 70s. It was then that the women started talking about things such as domestic violence and rape. A girl named Madhura was raped in a police station, and when the judiciary was lenient about it, it triggered widespread protests. Indian feminism took up issues such as dowry, female mortality, illiteracy among girls and women, and sexual violence. Some of these things were India-specific, the others were universal.

The third wave of Indian feminism started in 1990s, just like elsewhere. There was globalisation and liberalisation in India, which meant more financial independence for women. In the age of Internet and social media, Indian women too have seen more freedom and more empowerment. The traditional image of woman is being shattered. However, more freedom to women is bringing about its own set of problems. With more women being out on their own, there has been a steady rise in the rise of rapes in our society.

Think on it

1. What is cultural feminism?
    2. How is radical feminism different from liberal feminism?
    3. What is structural feminism?
    4. What is the relevance of postmodern feminism?
    5. Explain the three waves of feminism in India.

CHAPTER SEVENTEEN

Homosexuality

1. In simple societies

Simple societies display a wide range of permissiveness or restrictiveness toward homosexual relations. The Lepcha of the Himalayas viewed it with disgust. Because many societies deny homosexuality, little is known about it in them. Among the permissive ones, there is variation in the type and pervasiveness of homosexuality. In some societies, it is accepted to certain times and certain indivdiauls. Between 64 to 69 percent of simple societies tolerate homosexuality, with some of them even encouraging it (Gregersen, 1994).

The Berber-speaking Siwans of North Africa expected all males to engage in homosexual relations. Their custom limited a man to one boy. Such arrangments were made openly till 1909. And when these boys reached the age of 16 to 20 years, they married girls.

Among the Etoro of New Guinea, sex between husband and wife was prohibited for 260 days a year but there was no prohibition of homosexuality. They believed that a man's stock of semen was limited, and a man would die after it is exhausted. The boys could increase their stock of semen by getting it from older men through oral intercourse.

Evelyn Blackwood identified 95 societies with female-female homosexuality. Kaguru of Tanzania have female homosexual relationships between younger and older women as part of their initiation ceremonies.

Among the Azande of the Sudan, the unmarried warrior-age males, who lived apart from women for several years, had homosexual relations with the boys of the age grade of warrior apprentices.

Several reported cases of institutionalised lesbianism are related to the migration of males in search of work. On the Caribbean island of Carriacou, where migrant husbands stay away from home for most of the year, the older married women bring young single women to their households.

Polygynous marriage is another context in which lesbian relationships happen. The practice seems to have been common in Africa among Nupe, Hausa, Dahomy, Azande and Nayakysa.

It is extremely unusual to find exclusive homosexuality among males or females in simple societies.

2. In complex societies

What we understand from anthropology is that homosexuality had been prevalent in many simple societies. In our present-day society, it is a highly controversial topic. What do you make of homosexuality in our own society? You may know many things about it, you may have certain views. Is it a good thing or a bad thing? Is it just normal and natural or do you think it is really unnatural? Should things like homosexual marriages be allowed and legally sanctioned or should they be discouraged and banned?

You have to think about things and form some kind of opinions, and you must also not shy away from expressing your views. But you should also be prepared to modify your opinions in the light of new facts and new lines of reasoning. That is the way to study, not with a blank mind.

Some people tend to think that homosexuality is just a matter of individual choice. It is a person's choice and let him or her do what they want, as long as they are not hurting any other person. It is mostly a private and personal matter. The bisexual and homosexual people are not disturbing others, the state need not enter into their lives and so homosexuality should be decriminilised. In India, it had been criminalised since the British times till recently.

An important question here is: how do some people become homosexuals? One would think both genetic factors and upbringing come into play. There is some evidence that homosexuality is linked to genes. There is an area of the X chromosome that often looks the same in brothers who are gay. A study carried by Dean Hammer (1993) compared forty pairs of gay brothers and found that thirty-three shared an identical pattern of five DNA markers at the lower tip of the X chromosome.

In another study, Bailey and Pillard found that among 56 gay men who had identical twins, 52% of the co-twins were gay. Among 54 gay men who had fraternal twins, 22% of the co-twins were gay. Among gay men who had adoptive brothers, only 11% of the adoptive brothers were gay. Among 71 lesbians who had identical twins, 48% of the co-twins were lesbian. Among 37 lesbians who had fraternal twins, 16% of the co-twins were lesbian. Among lesbians who had adoptive sisters, only 6% of the adoptive siblings were lesbian.

A major difference between simple and complex societies in matters of homosexuality is that in simple societies there are nothing like the gay clubs and gay rights movements. Homosexuality exists but it is almost never exclusive. Exclusive homosexual orientation in large numbers of people seems to be only a feature of complex societies.

In simple societies, people may have homosexual relations besides normal heterosexual relations. Typically, isolated men who don't have access to women tend to have homosexual relations with other men. Similarly, when there are not many men around, women tend to have homosexual relationships with other women. But in normal circumstances, when men and women are living together in a society, there would be no homosexuality.

I strongly suspect that no one is an exclusive gay or an exclusive lesbian by nature. All of us seem to have tendencies for homosexuality in different degrees. It is just that some people because of their positive experience with the people of same sex or negative experience with the people of opposite sex may be freezing their orientation. I am making a hypothesis. You are free to accept or reject.

The people who claim to be completely heterosexual with absolutely no homosexual tendencies have the capacity to be homosexual under certain circumstances. Also, the people who claim to be exclusively homosexual may show heterosexual tendencies in some situations.

Human sexuality has a wide range and we are capable of many things sexually. The process of socialisation contributes to limiting the range of one's sexual preferences and orientation. Kin relations tend to curb our sexual tendencies. In South India, you are supposed to be attracted to your cross-cousin, whereas in North India, you are not supposed to feel sexually attracted to any cousin. In fact, the entire culture is about taming our sexual instinct. Don't you think so?

What is meant by a good girl in the conventional sense? What is the Hindu concept of chastity in an ideal woman? What is the Sharia code about Muslim women? They are all ways to control the free and natural expression of a woman's sexuality. Woman is restricted far more than man in any society, but a man too is severely limited sexually. By nature, our sexuality is a huge part of our being. It is not confined to one person or one particular relationship. We go about curtailing and curbing ourselves, repressing our sexual nature.

Evolutionary biologists like Richard Dawkins explored how these people who manifest exclusive homosexuality escaped elimination by evolution. The emergence of exclusive homosexuality – gays and lesbians as a category of people – is probably an outcome of sexual restrictiveness and the culture of labelling. It is due to not seeing in oneself the range of sexual possibilities and identifying oneself with a specific orientation and makigng it a matter of identity. But a lot more research is needed to be done on this subject.

Think on it

1. Is there homosexuality in simple societies?

2. Are there people who label themselves 'gays' and 'lesbians' in simple societies?

3. Are there genetic factors in homosexuality? Explain.

4. Why do only complex societies seem to have exclusive homosexuality?

CHAPTER EIGHTEEN

Transgender Issues

Transgender issues in our times are quite serious. Transgender and homosexual people are often grouped under the LGBT or LGBTQ community. It stands for Lesbians, Gays, Bisexuals, Transgender; when Q is added to LBGT, it refers to Queer or Questioning. Together, they represent the people of alternative gender and sexual orientation. But I would say that this term LGBT could be misleading. By clumping transgender people with homosexual people, we may not be showing the transgender community the kind of attention and response that it requires.

Transgender is a very serious biological issue. According to Anne Fausto-Sterling (1993), there are at least five biological sexes:

1. Males: individuals born with two testes and male genitalia

2. Females: individuals born with two ovaries and female genitalia

3. Male pseudohermaphrodites: individuals who have two testes, no ovaries, but a mix of male and female genitalia

4. Female pseudohermaphrodites: individuals who have two ovaries, no testes, but a mix of male and female genitalia

5. Hermaphrodites: individuals born with one testis, one ovary and a mix of male and female genitalia; some of them have a penis and a vagina large enough that they can have sex with a normal man or woman.

The above classification refers only to bodily differences, when we consider the mind factor, things become even more complicated. A normal-looking girl can feel like a boy inside and vice versa. When a transgender child is born, the male genitalia can be seen but not the ovaries that are inside the body. The parents would think he is a boy and he would grow up as a boy. But as he grows up, he may see many female characteristics in his ways of thinking and behaviour. His parents and the people around him may notice something odd about him. Sex is not just about the physical body.

Transgender people who have gone through a lot of personal trauma say that the female mind is intrinsically different from the male mind. Voice, breasts, hair, facial appearance, body size – there are many such external physical differences between males and females, besides the genitalia; in addition, males and females differ from each other fundamentally in their mental makeup.

A transgender child lives through the agony of a deep identity crisis as he or she grows up. The boys will say to him or her, ”You are like a girl,” and the girls will say, “You are like a boy.” Where an interviewer asked a transgender person regarding the time when she realised she is a transgendered person, she replied, “I did not realise it, I was told so. I was made to realise that I was not normal. I did not realise it by myself.”

Sometimes the doctor might see the gender mix-up. Then the doctor has to go by his judgement – who is the child more likely to be, male or female? Is it a boy or a girl? The doctor might think it would be a girl and remove the penis and other things. But as the child grows up and reaches puberty, she might realise she is a boy, because many bodily changes and the way she feels within do not match with being a girl.

The parents and doctors may have to make important choices about the gender of the child. But even if a child is surgically corrected, she or he may not grow to be a normal male or a normal female, because the fact of being a male or a female is not confined to the genitalia.

Isn't this issue much different from homosexuality? Sociologists should make a study of homosexual and transgender people based on the socio-economic classes they belong to. Homosexual people are almost always from the upper classes. They discover their sexual preferences and they make it a matter of rights. A transgender person may belong to any class and he or she is likely to face much economic and social discrimination throughout life. Particularly in a developing country like India, he or she will face many education and livelihood issues. Even now in most application forms for education and employment, there are only the gender categories of male and female, there is no third.

In India there has been a tradition of giving a specific role to a hijra, a transgender person. Hijras form communities of their own. They have their own leaders. Typically, they go around in small groups, singing and clapping loudly. They seek to bless others, in return for payment.It was believed by many that their blessings had power. That was tradition. Now their coming to bless is regarded more as a harassment.

The hijras are not given any jobs in our society. They have to beg for a living. Oddly enough, some of them make money by being sex workers. A transgender sex worker said, "Whatever kind of sex that men can't get from their wives, they demand it from us; all kind of sexual activities." So it is a life long discrimination – for which they are not responsible.

If a person is both a man and a woman, why should he or she be discriminated against? The transgender issue is about biological ambiguity, which also manifests as psychological ambiguity. But the society is not able to face the gender ambiguity.

Recently the Parliament has passed a bill mandating the state to recognise the third gender. Soon, admission forms and applications will be provided with this option.

How should a good society deal with the issue of transgender? A society should first recognise that male and female are not the only genders that exist. There is a third. Furthermore, the sex of a person with ambiguity should not be determined by the opinion of others but by the person himself or herself, because a lot of it depends upon the subjective feeling of what one is.

We may feel comfortable with people of regular male or female gender, but tend to feel ill at ease with people of mixed gender. We normally have a very fixed view of the genders, whereas nature sometimes produces complications. We discriminate against the transgender people. A person in female dress and male body with male voice may confuse and even scare us. But if we know about their problems and plight, if we realise how much they are discriminated against, then we are likely to be more considerate towards them.

Section 377 of the Indian Penal Code condemns and criminalises all "unnatural sex." This section was being used to persecute the LGBT community. Recently it has been annulled. The LGBT community have more freedom now in this country. As a society, we have a narrow perspective not only of gender but of sex too – things have to be only in this way and not any other. When it comes to transgender, different kinds of sex are possible. Criminalising what was considered unnatural sex by the British people during the colonial times paved way for much police harassment for the people of the LGBT community. All that would be stopped now.

The transgender issue raises and partly answers the question of what it really means to be a man or a woman. In one movie the hero was saying, ,there are men and woman. But there is nothing like man's mind and woman's mind.' This doesn't seem to be true. There is man's mind as well as woman's mind.

Currently in advanced countries, when a child is born with a noticeable sexual ambiguity, a medical screening committee will look into what can be done; to make the child more of a boy or a girl, or not to do anything about it.

Human rights activists are asking: "Why do you want to force everyone into two genders? If a person can have sex with both man and woman, what is wrong?" The activists are saying that we should not think narrowly and human possibilities are many.

When a doctor is asked, "Why do you want to fix the gender this way or that way, why don't you leave as it is?" he says, "The parents are concerned. The parents want their child to either be a boy or a girl. And they want to settle it before others know that there is a problem with the child." When the parents know that there is an ambiguity and they want to remove that ambiguity, it becomes a struggle for the transgender children. Their struggle starts from their own homes.

Terms

1. Lesbian: a woman whose enduring physical, romantic, and/or emotional attraction is to other women. Some lesbians may prefer to identify as gay or as gay women.

2. Gay: the adjective used to describe people whose enduring physical, romantic and/or emotional attractions are to people of the same sex. Sometimes lesbian is the preferred term for women.

3. Bisexual: a person who has the capacity to form enduring physical, romantic, and/or emotional attractions to those of the same gender or to those of another gender.

4. Transgender: an umbrella term for people whose gender identity and/or gender expression differs from what is typically associated with the sex they were assigned at birth.

5. Queer: an adjective used by some people, particularly young people, whose sexual orientation is not exclusively heterosexual. Typically, for those who identify as queer, the terms lesbian, gay and bisexual are perceived to be too limiting and/or fraught with cultural connotations they feel don't apply to them. However, this is not universally accepted term even within the LGBT community.

6. Questioning: sometimes, Q can mean questioning. The term describes someone who is questioning their gender identity or sexual orientation.

Think on it

1. What is Q in LGBTQ?
   2. How many types of transgender people are possible?

3. What is the difference in the issues that transgenders face compared to homosexuals?

4. How was Section 377 relevant to the transgender people?

5. What social reforms are needed to help the lives of the transgender people?

Movie Review: Super Deluxe

Super Deluxe, a 2019 Tamil film directed by Thiagarajan Kumararaja, covers three stories with some interesting characters and ideas. Here, we will just look into the main story with the transgender theme.

Raasu Kutti, a six year old boy, is waiting for his dad to return. The father abandoned the family even before the child was born, and now he called them to say he is coming back. Kutti is keen to show his dad to his friends in the school because he hated being called a 'test tube baby'. Some relatives join Kutti and his mom, Jyothi, to receive Kutti's dad.

A saree-clad woman, with a well-built manly body, gets down from the taxi, to the perplexity of everyone. Kutti's dad, Manickam, has came back as a woman, Shilpa (Vijay Sethupathi in female form). She walks in.

Jyothi is confused and is in tears. Soon she gets to watch her husband put on a saree, make up and a wig. She does not know which is better between having an absconding husband and having a weird man-turned-woman for a husband.

The kid, however, is determined to show his dad to his friends in the school. On the way to the school, he asks his dad many questions. His dad explains, "I was brought up as a man, but I always wanted to be a woman, so I went to Bombay and got myself changed into a woman. Just the way we put the left foot in the right shoe by mistake, God put me, a woman, in a man's body.'

On the first day itself, Shilpa realizes how harsh this world is for a transgender like her. In men's bathroom, when she is helping Kutti zip up the pants, a security guard mistakes her to be a pedophile, beats her up and hands her over to the police. At the police station, she is forced to perform a demeaning sexual act for the SI. When she finally reaches the school, she is not allowed inside. Kutti shows her to his friends from a distance. His friends laugh, saying, "How can she be your dad? You are indeed a test tube baby!"

At times, people refer to her by a neuter gender – as if she is some subhuman entity. When she is walking on the road, people around her pass snide comments. She gets insulted before her son. Feeling that she would be a liability to her son, she decides to go back to Bombay and never to return.

Shilpa bids adieu to Kutti, saying, "My son, live well. Earn respect of others. Remember, to earn respect, you should be like others. Blend with them. If you are unique, they will fear you. When they fear you, they start hating you.'

But Kutti is devastated when he gets to know his dad is going to abandon him again. This is something that Shilpa did not expect. She is touched by Kutti's words: "Whatever you want, you be that. Be a man, or a be a woman. It is your choice. It does not matter to us. You are my dad. I and my mother want you." Kutti's unconditional love melts Shilpa, she changes her mind and stays back with the family.

CHAPTER NINETEEN

Evolutionary Psychology of Sex and Gender

Much of the activism and writing related to gender issues emphasizes the evils of gender hierarchy and proposes ways to reduce this hierarchy. There is, unfortunately, less discussion on what in fact constitute the real differences between men and women, and even less discussion on how to address them. Should we try to reduce the differences or should we try to enhance them? In their bid for gender equality, many feminists try to overlook the actual differences that exist between the sexes. But the differences are real and we should first understand them so that we can try to do something about them. What is the ideal path of growth for a man, for a woman, and for their relationship? This is not an easy question to answer. In looking for answers, it helps if we first understand the differences in the desires of men and women. What do they want from each other?

In his book *The Evolution of Desire,* David M. Buss lists the differences between what women want from their mates and what men want. He traces the roots of their desires to the evolutionary past of the species. Here we present a summary of his findings.

1. What women want

Levels of desire

Men are more casual about sex, but women tend to be much more choosy and discriminating. Man's emotional investment both in the act and its possible outcome is much less compared to that of woman. Men produce millions of sperm, which are replenished at a rate of 12 million per hour. Women produce a fixed lifetime supply of 1 to 2 million ova. Of these, only 400 mature to be capable of fertilized. Woman's involvement in sex may not end with the act itself; if she is impregnated, she would have to carry the child for nine months, and after delivery, she would have to breast-feed the child and constantly take care of her son or daughter for at least three to four years.

Because of such differences, men generally want much more sex than women. When men want to have more and women are being choosy, this creates a ground for conflict between the sexes. It can be one explanation for sexual violence.

How do we know that these differences in the levels of investment can lead to differences in the levels of desire? The male mormon cricket produces a large 'spermatophore' that comes loaded with nutrients. The females compete for the male crickets. There is a reversal of sex roles. In all such sex-role reversed species, the males tend to be choosy about sex and the females are more aggressive and larger than the males. But in more than 5000 species of mammals, including more than 250 primate species, it is the females who bear the burden of internal fertilisation, gestation and lactation. So is it with humans as well. Do you think this may explain to some extent why boys usually chase girls and why the girls may want to be chased rather than themselves chasing the boys?

Men with resources

That women want men with resources may appear obvious. But the gender gap in this aspect is not so obvious. Women value men with resources much more than men value women with resources. This is a universal pattern. A study of 10,000 individuals in 37 cultures on six continents and five islands that varied on many cultural parameters showed this to be true.

In a 1939 study, women in America valued good financial prospects in a mate twice as highly as men valued women with good financial background. This finding was replicated in 1956 and again in 1967. Buss surveyed around 1500 Americans in the mid-1980s using the same questionnaire. The result turned out to be the same. Even the studies done in 2015 support the premise. Sexual revolutions and the spread of feminism did not seem to alter what women want. They still want from their men what they wanted decades ago!

Why is it so? Intrinsically, a woman seeks a man who can take care of her children. She has historically evolved offering sex in exchange for resources for themselves and their children.

Consider a bird called gray shrike. Just before the start of the breeding season, male shrikes begin amassing caches of 90 to 120 items of prey, such as snails, and other useful objects, such as pieces of cloth. They put these items on display. Females prefer the males with the largest caches. When biologist Reuven Yosef removed portions of some males' caches and added some items to the caches of others, the females shifted to the males with larger bounties. The female birds entirely avoided the males without any resources.

Human females have evolved to be more attracted to males with greater resources or resource potential. It means preference for men with higher education, higher salary, higher intelligence and higher status. It also indirectly means higher age, because generally one's resources increase with one's age.

How about women who already have enough resources, what would their preferences be? Cross-cultural studies show women with their own resources value resources in a potential mate even more than women lacking in resources, and not less. This has been found among women in Spain, Jordan, Serbia, and England.

While women may complain about domination by men, they in fact tend to choose men who are superior to them and who can dominate them. Is not there a contradiction in the desire structure of women?

Athletic bodies

Women prefer tall, strong, athletic bodies among potential mates. They also have a specific preference for the V-shaped torso, i.e., broader shoulders relative to hips. Modern men show upper body strength that is roughly twice that of women. Broader shoulders is one of most sexually dimorphic attributes of the human body. The female preference could have influenced the evolution of the male body.

Men should be more manly, looking more different from the women. Some attractive masculine features are associated with higher levels of testosterone in the body, which can however be bad for the health of these men. These pronounced masculine features can only be good if the men have a strong immune system.

Why do women desire men with strong, athletic bodies? Because men are expected to protect women from other men. Among gladiator frogs, the males are responsible for creating nests and defending the eggs. In the majority of courtships, a stationary male is deliberately bumped by a female who is considering him. She strikes him with great force. Most females mate only with those males who move minimally when bumped.

Among baboons, the females form a special friendship with the males who offer physical protection to them and their infants. In return, the females give them sexual access.

In everything that a woman does in the mating process, she has unconsciously or instinctively the protection and well-being of herself and her present or future children as a central concern. She gets these things from man, in return for which she provides sex, something that man craves for.

Love

For a woman, it is not enough if man has the strength and the resources, he should come to her and only her. His resources should not be diverted to other females. If this has to be assured, he should love her and only her. Love brings certainty to the flow of resources to her side. Therefore, women place much more value on love than men do.

2. *What Men Want*

Beauty

What constitutes beauty? Why are some women regarded more beautiful than others? Is there any objective criterion? Or is beauty only in the eye of the beholder? Or could the notions of beauty be culturally conditioned?

When psychologist Michael Cunningham (1989) asked people of different races to judge the facial attractiveness of women of various races in photographs, he found great consensus among Asian and American men about who was and was not good-looking. Other researchers found similar consensus among the Chinese, Indian and English subjects, between South Africans and Americans, and between Black Americans and White Americans. This finding may not surprise you. Did you find heroines in foreign movies unattractive? Less likely. This is so because of the commonality of perception regarding what is beautiful.

Symmetry

Symmetrical faces among both men and women are considered more attractive. Psychologist Steve Gangestad and biologist Randy Thornhill examined the relationship between symmetry and attractiveness. They found environmentally induced injuries and diseases produce asymmetries during physical development. Parasites and genetic mutations also cause asymmetry. Symmetry is a clue to health. Moreover, asymmetry increases with age, so symmetry is also a measure of youth.

In scorpionflies, swallows and many other species, males prefer to mate with symmetric females and tend to avoid those that asymmetries.

Large and firm breasts

Men in many cultures prefer women with large and firm breasts. Men are obsessed about breasts. From an evolutionary point of view, big breasts are attractive because they provide clues to the reproductive capacity of women.

Only a very few cultures are an exception to this. Among the Azande of Sudan and the Ganda of Uganda, men find long and pendulous breasts more attractive. When there is such a variation, it may be helpful to see why is it so.

Smaller waist

A study done by psychologist Devendra Singh shows that, across cultures, men find women with a smaller waist size relative to hip size attractive. Before puberty, boys and girls show a similar fat distribution over the body. At puberty, boys lose fat from their buttocks and thighs, while the release of estrogens in pubescent girls causes the fat in their bodies to be deposited primarily on their hips and upper thighs. The volume of the body fat in this region is 40% greater for women than for men.

Women with lower waist-to-hip ratio show earlier pubertal endocrine activity. Women with a higher ratio may have some difficulty in becoming pregnant; those who become do so at a later age. The waist-to-hip ratio among women is also an accurate indicator of their long-term health status.

Singh found women with a ratio of 0.7 to be more attractive than women with a ratio of 0.8, who in turn are more attractive than women with a ratio of 0.9. Singh's analysis of Playboy centrefolds and winners of beauty contests in the US over 30 consecutive years corroborate this finding. Although both centrefolds and beauty contest winners got thinner, their waist-to-hip ratio remained roughly the same at around 0.7.

Slimness

The most culturally variable standard of beauty seems to be the preference for a slim figure over a plump figure. In cultures where food is scarce, such as the Bushmen of Australia, plumpness signals health and adequate nutrition. In cultures where food is abundant, as in the US and many European countries, plumpness is not regarded as attractive as slimness.

Studies by Paul Rozin show there is a communication gap between men and women on this issue of size. American women were asked to indicate their ideal shape for themselves as well as their perception of men's ideal female figure. When men were asked which female figure they preferred, they selected the one with average body size. It seems like American women erroneously believe that men desire thinner women more than they actually do.

Physical attractiveness

Multiple long-term mating studies in the US from 1939 to 1996 show that men rate physical attractiveness and good looks as more important in a potential mate than do women. Men's greater preference for physically attractive mates is among the most consistently documented psychological sex differences.

In the US, the importance attached to good looks in a marriage partner on a scale of 0.00 to 3.00 increased between 1939 and 1989 from 1.50 to 2.11 for men and from 0.94 to 1.67 for women. Similar shifts have been observed in China, India and Brazil in the more recent decades. This shows that even when preferences in selecting a mate change, the gap between men and women remains the same.

Youth

In studies done from 1939 to 2005, American students have always preferred women younger than themselves. Man's preoccupation with a woman's youth is universal. No society is an exception to this. An international study that examined 37 societies has reiterated this point. The variation between the societies is only in terms of the preferred age difference. On average, men preferred women two and half years younger.

As men get older, they prefer women increasingly younger than they are. Younger women are preferred because of their reproductive value. As men age, the difference between them and the women they want increases. Desirability is associated with reproductive value. Boys aged 15 years tend to prefer older girls of 17 or 18 years.

Virginity and fidelity

The fact of men valuing premarital chastity more than women holds up worldwide but cultures vary in the value they place on virginity. People in China, India, Indonesia, Iran, Taiwan and Palestine attach a higher value on virginity compared to many other countries. For people in Sweden, Norway, Finland, the Netherlands, Germany and France, virginity in a potential mate is unimportant. In the US, the value of virginity declined over the last 70 years.

Economic independence of women is a very important variable affecting the value of virginity. When women are independent, the general levels of premarital sex in a society go up. After all, men can't demand virginity, when they can not get. By nature, men abhor promiscuity and infidelity in their wives. Unfaithfulness seems to be more upsetting to men than any other pain their spouses can inflict on them. Promiscuous girls are not desired as long term mates. The single best predictor of extramarital sex is premarital sexual permissiveness.

The evolutionary basis of man's desires is about how best to perpetuate his genes. Women should be reproductively successful as well as faithful.

Man wants status too through his mate, a factor which influences his choice. But in this respect, the desire of man is akin to that of woman.

Think on it

1. What do women want when selecting a mate?

2. Can you say evolution of males is influenced by female preferences?

3. What do men want when selecting a mate?

4. Can you list the most important differences between sexes in terms of what they value in a mate?

CHAPTER TWENTY

Forms of Religion

What is religion? **Religion** refers to any set of attitudes, beliefs, and practices pertaining to a supernatural power, whether that power rests in forces, gods, spirits, ghosts or demons. What is supernatural? **Supernatural** refers to powers believed to be non-human or not subject to the laws of nature.

The essence of all religions lies in a belief in the supernatural. A religion need not be a belief in a god. A belief in a god is religion but a religion need not involve a belief in a god. There can be a belief in one God, or there can be a belief in many gods and spirits. **Monotheism** refers to believing that there is only one God and that all other supernatural beings are subordinate to, or are alternative manifestations of this supreme being. **Polytheism** refers to recognising many gods, none of whom is believed to be superordinate.

A belief in ghosts, spirits, and souls – all this is religion. All the phenomena associated with the supernatural dimension come under religion. Does Ram Gopal Varma make movies on religion? You wouldn't think he does, but indeed he does because he makes films on ghosts. Everything associated with any supernatural element actually comes under religion.

1. Religion is universal

The question is – why may we be interested in the supernatural at all? Why don't we confine ourselves to what is natural? Natural is something observable, verifiable, and empirical. What do you want to do with this thing called the supernatural? Why do you want to be engaged with it? Be it gods, ghosts or spirits. Why? Is it an inherent part of the human nature?

Why do we want to relate to *the* supernatural? Take a seemingly mundane thing like your civil services exam. Where do you place it? Natural or supernatural? Some may associate it with the supernatural, because something unpredictable that is not in their hands could happen. I will ask more specifically, do you hold any supernatural beliefs about yourselves? Look within and answer.

You might say no, you may think your belief in certain things is natural but the person next to you may think your belief is supernatural. The answer may startle you but ask the person next to you, do you think I will clear the exam? Does he think you will? Is it likely or unlikely ? We have been struggling to clear the exam, but sometimes the people around us may think we wouldn't make it. They may have many reasons to think so. But then we are guided and motivated by one single desire: to clear the exam. They may think though that unless some supernatural intervention takes place, you would not be able to get through. Doesn't it show that what is natural to you can be supernatural to another person?

Or you yourself may realise , yes, my idea of clearing the exam is supernatural and that supernatural is a part of me. Supernatural doesn't have to mean flying in air all by oneself. It can simply mean just clearing this exam. Not only do we want to clear the exam, we also want to do so many things after that. We want to enter politics, we want to transform the society. We want to turn the globe upside down and we think we can do it!

All those beliefs, we keep to ourselves, deeply hidden. The maximum we do is that we say that we are preparing for the exam, we do not say we want to turn the world upside down. If we say any such thing, they may think we are crazy. But then, we continue to dream.

Do we think only rationally? Are our actions based solely on reason? Or are they based on fantasies, myths – equivalent to flying in air without any means? They may look supernatural to others but they may be quite natural to us.

We go by our fantasies. But this is not to say that we should not have a fantasy. After all, how are we different from the people around us? It is only by the reach of our fantasies. Otherwise externally we are doing the same things, eating, sleeping, coming to the class, reading. We are only different because of our fantasies! They raise us above the ordinary.

We are not dreaming of flying in the air without any machine, we dream of other things. In every one of us, there is a non-rational part that may be the essence of our existence. That may be our soul. That is what defines us.

We hold it precious and we tend to be secretive about it. If you come across somebody who accepts your fantasies and the things that the you believe in , then probably you will fall in love with that person. Love may be about accepting each other's fantasies. If a person looks at you in the way everyone else looks at you, you won't feel special; but if the other person looks at you in a way that you look at yourself, then that is a different kind of acceptance.

The idea that we are completely rational, that we always go by a reasoning, that we always think logically is not at all true. The logical and rational side is a part of us, the non-logical and non-rational side is another part of us. And it is good if you accept your non-rationality while also accepting others' non-rationality. You have your dreams, and you respect others' dreams and you don't say that those dreams do not have any basis.

The non-rational is what may be guiding us. You can call it a myth. We have myths about ourselves. It is not at all an unhealthy thing to believe in myths. Life is extremely mundane, routine and meaningless without a belief in the myths.

Imagine what you want to do with your life. It is a myth – the core of it. You say you want to serve people but then ask yourself further why you want to do it. Then some other myth comes. Just like individuals have myths about themselves, societies also have. Societies also have non-rational parts. What is rational to one society may look superstitious or irrational to others.

Essentially, neither individuals nor societies go solely by reason, being completely limited by it. Because reason doesn't have much depth to it. Going beyond reason is entering a vast space with many possibilities. Many explorations can happen.

Anthropologists are keenly interested in studying that part of the society that is called religion. Then they are also interested in finding out the link between that part and other aspects of the society. Just like your myth is guiding you and driving you – what is the myth of a particular society and how does it guide it? Myth is not used in a negative sense here. The non-rational aspect is a part of life, part of an individual life, part of social life. All the non-rational aspects, be it gods, spirits, ghosts, souls and the people who practise them, priests, magicians, shamans – all are studied under this phenomenon called religion. There has never been any society without a religion. You can go to the most primitive society or take the most advanced society, there has not been a society without a religion because the supernatural is there inside every individual.

The non-rational and mythical part is there in every one of us. It may be that some people have more of it. People who have less of it may be called pragmatic, people who have more of it may be called visionaries. But you don't come across anybody who does not have any non-rational aspect at all in his personality. Some people think of things which others cannot dream, they are predisposed to think like that, while some are more down to earth and more pragmatic.

The religion that a society produces makes use of this non-rational part in every one of us. We have the propensity to dream, to think of higher things, not to confine ourselves to the mundane. Religious phenomena deal with something beyond the mundane, beyond the materialistic, beyond the rational – the other side of reason by which man has always been fascinated. There is a connection between the other side and this side. There are some people who function as intermediaries between the two.

There is the mundane world and there is something beyond it. How do some people negotiate this gap? Here comes the role of the religious specialists. They may have particular skills, they may have particular predispositions. They deal with the supernatural with greater ease and tell the people that this is what it is. Religion is not simply a matter of dogma or a belief system, it is something more. Religion may have superstition, may have dogma, but it is not only that, it is much more.

Consider a bus accident in which many people died. You can explain it in terms of how it took place, but you can't explain why it should have taken place. If the bus had stopped earlier for two minutes at some place, that accident would not have happened. Some say all those things that led to the accident happened to make it happen. And furthermore, an amulet can perhaps protect you against such things, according to them. If you were one of the passengers, your life could have been spared.

Hinduism may give a specific explanation for this kind of thing. It happened in this way because it was predestined to happen in this way. It is all written in some sense. This is called karma. These are all answers given to the question of why something should have happened in a particular way. Because many possibilities exist.

Religion enters when other explanations fail. You can explain something naturally, through a particular line of causation. But you can't explain why it should have happened in that way only when there are many other possibilities. Man is not in a habit of saying, 'Okay, I don't know'. If he was in a position to say 'I do not know', much of religion may not have happened.

When the natural explanations fail, something else comes into the picture. One of the functions of religion is to explain what can't be explained exclusively by natural causes.

2. Animism

Religion is universal, but the nature of religious belief is cultural. The religions of simple societies are different from those of complex societies. Animism is a commonly seen religion in simple societies. **Animism** refers to a belief in dual existence for all things

– a physical, visible body, and a psychic, invisible soul.

It was first proposed by E.B. Tylor that simple societies believe in souls and such a belief in souls was the earliest form of religion. He thought the primitive man came up on this idea of soul after observing certain natural phenomena like sleep and dreams. During sleep, a man goes into a dream and visits many places. After he gets up, he wonders where went. Then, Tylor reasoned, the primitive man must have thought that something went out of him and that was the soul. Dream is something where the soul goes out of the body and comes back. Death is something where the soul goes out of the body and does not come back. Then the primitive man must have thought that just like humans have souls, other life forms also may have souls. There is something physical and there is something non-physical.

It is true that many societies believed in souls, in something non-physical. Does Hinduism believe in soul? Very much. And what is supposed to happen to the soul after a person's death? Lord Krishna in the Bhagavad Gita says that only bodies die, the souls do not. They simply enter new bodies. That is the Hindu belief of souls. Marvin Harris points out that there are widely varying types of beliefs about the souls among different religions. Ancient Egyptians believed that a person has two souls. The Dahomey of West Africa say that women have three souls and men have four. Different simple and complex societies have different kind of beliefs about the nature of the human soul, but the belief in the existence of the soul is widely prevalent.

3.Animatism

The soul is specific to a person or an entity. It is the non-physical dimension of the physical form. That is what Tylor proposed that early men believed. But R. Marett suggested that the early form of religious belief might not have been in souls, rather it was in some kind of impersonal force. This belief system is called **animatism,**referring to a belief in supernatural forces.

Some objects may carry these impersonal forces, some people may carry the impersonal force. Do we have those beliefs now that some objects may be carrying some force? Like in the things we wear. Amulets, charms or certain kind of rings are believed to protect a person who wears or carries them.

Animatism is also called manaism after the term 'mana' used by Melanesians to call this force. This belief is also found among the Munda and the Ho. Among the Ho, the impersonal power is called bonga. Bonga is the cause of all energy. They believe that even modern-day things like a bicycle, a steam engine, and an aeroplane have all bonga is varying degrees. Differences in individuals in regard to their power or prestige are due to the differences in the degree of bonga that is present in them.

4. Naturism

Naturism refers to the belief that the forces of nature have supernatural power. Max Muller advocated that the most ancient form of religious practice is naturism. Man develops dependency, fear, and respect with regard to the forces of nature. The first religious experience came out of a personification of the forces of nature. The worshipping of the forces of nature during the early Vedic times is an example of naturism. Wind, sun, fire, and water were personified and worshipped.

5. Fetishism

A **fetish** is an object imbued with ritual potency; often surrounded with taboos and conferring material benefits upon its keeper. In the early part of the 16th century, when the Portuguese were exploring West Coast Africa, they found the natives using small material objects in their religious worship.

Auguste Comte considered fetishism as a part of the theological stage of world history, along with polytheism and monotheism. He considered naturism also as a part of fetishism. But this theory was later cast aside. Tylor made fetishism a subdivision of animism. But this view also can be set aside as the spirit in the fetish is not the same as the soul.

Fritz Schultze, a German philosopher, says that fetishism is a worship of material objects. Believers look at them as alive and sentient, and tend to connect them with auspicious and inauspicious events. Stones, bows, gores, and stripes can sometimes be fetish objects. Schultze says that fetishism is a part of the primitive religion, but not the whole of it. The primitive people may worship spirits too. Schultze holds the view that man ceases to be a fetish-worshipper as soon as he learns to distinguish the spirit from the material object.

A fetish differs from an amulet which is a pledge of protection from a divine power. A fetish has divine power within it. A fetish is not an idol, which is a representation of a divine power. Some anthropologists do not make this distinction – for example, church relics, crucifixes, and copies of the Bible are seen as fetishes imbued with power by the believers, according to some anthropologists. But fetishes are typically small objects while idols like a crucifix are bigger.

6. Attitude towards ghosts

Most societies have a belief in ghosts and spirits. The society's attitude towards ghosts is also an aspect of its culture. What could be our attitude towards ghosts in the modern-day world? Would we be scared or would we be delighted if we see a ghost? Most likely, we would be scared. It seems this fear of ghosts is more of an European phenomenon. In the ancient cultures, ghosts were not always feared.

Probably the prevalent fear of ghosts in our times is because of the movies and the Western influence. Director Ram Gopal Varma made many movies with ghosts in them, but the ghosts probably wouldn't like the scary way in which he presented them. He did not make a movie where there are kind and good ghosts which help people. There can also be movies about the good ghosts fighting the bad ghosts. Why has Ram Gopal Varma not made any movies about the good ghosts – when he himself would become a ghost, the ghosts may take up this issue with him!

Nowadays we fear even the ghosts of the departed people who are near and dear to us. But traditionally it had not been so. If your grandfather died, his soul is something that you may want to see. In China it is believed that the ghosts and souls of the ancestors are supposed to protect a family. Some societies have friendly attitude towards the non-rational elements such as ghosts and souls. But we are now moving towards a situation where we only get totally scared and frightened of them. This is not necessary. There can be friendly ghosts and friendly souls, just some of the ghosts are unfriendly. With the friendly ghosts, you can ask them favours, whereas with the unfriendly ones, you would need to placate them. The friendly ones and the unfriendly ones may have a fight. Religion in simple societies involves such beliefs. It would be difficult for us to think in that way, but we can still cultivate a little friendly attitude.

The clear distinction between the natural and supernatural is a modern phenomenon. In modern societies, the gods are very distant from the people. In simple societies, the gods are felt to be much closer. In simple societies, the gods closely guide people. You can talk to your grandparents regarding their attitude towards gods, you may sense less distance between them and their gods. And this is just a difference between the people of three generations. For many of you, the gods may be relevant only just before an exam. You may pray – hoping they will help, in case anyone is there. It is not something that is done with any conviction. But a few generations ago, people had more serious beliefs about the supernatural. The gods were guiding the people, giving directions through signs. A cat comes, it could be a sign. A lizard falls at a particular spot on the body, it could be a sign. Somebody above is telling you not to do something. There was a closer connection with the realm of the supernatural.

7. Religion and magic

Anthropology makes a distinction between religion and magic. Both religion and magic deal with the supernatural, but a distinction is made between them. Those who make the distinction say that religion deals with request, prayer, uncertainty while magic deals with command and has some certainty to it. In religion, people pray to the supernatural, "God, please help!" The outcome of the request is uncertain. In magic, people believe that if a ritual process is done properly, the desired outcome is almost certain. Magic has a touch of certainty to it.

Magic refers to the performance of certain rituals that are believed to compel the supernatural powers to act in particular ways. **Rituals** are repetitive sets of behaviour that occur in essentially the same patterns every time they occur. Magic rituals and religious rituals involve in invoking the supernatural in some way.

James George Frazer, a famous anthropologist, believed that societies first develop a belief in magic. They would think they can control the supernatural in a particular way. Then they come to realise that they are not able to do it, and then religion is born. Much later, they will get to know that while there are many things that cannot be controlled, there are many other things that can be controlled directly by humans, and then science and technology are born. Frazer thought of religion in evolutionary terms. Societies have magic first, then they have religion, and then they come to science.

Malinowski however said that societies tend to have all these three elements at the same time, it is not that one gives rise to another and disappears. He noted that the inhabitants of the Trobriand Islands are good at making boats, they know the science of them, but they can't understand why a storm comes at a particular moment and why particular boats are sunk. So they resort to the supernatural too.

Take our society, where is the element of magic in our society? Witchcraft, sorcery, 'chetabadi' – they still happen in some villages of our country. If the procedure of magic is followed properly, then a good result is expected to come. In sorcery and witchcraft, evil outcomes are expected, but magic need not be always evil and negative, it can be positive too. If you do a certain ritual while chanting some mantras, positive outcomes are expected, the spirits will help you. The spirits could also harm another person in order to help you.

Another difference between magic and religion is that while magic is mostly personal, religion takes on a social aspect. A temple, a priest, a group identity, such are the elements of religion. In magic, individuals want to influence the supernatural for their personal ends. Religion has a collective character also, while magic does not.

Going by Frazer's view of the evolution of religion, what happens to the elements of magic, religion and science as societies become more modernised? Between magic and religion, isn't the element of magic reducing and the religious component increasing? Between religion and science, the element of science increases. There is some truth in Frazer's view. Magic is less, religion is more and then science is much more in our modern society. In this perspective, as science increases, what happens to religion? It diminishes.

Frazer found that magic is based on two principles: 1) like produces like 2) once in contact, always in contact. The first is based on the law of similarity, the magic associated with it is called homoeopathic, imitative or memetic magic. The second is based on the law of contact or contagion, the magic associated with it is called contagious magic.

In the Chota Nagpur region of India, some tribes associate thunder with rain. When they want rain, they sacrifice a hen or a pig, and fling stones and rocks down the hill. Through rolling the stones, they are producing something similar to thunder. Thunder should follow. With thunder, rain should happen. The Ho produce clouds of smoke to get rain. Real clouds should follow. With clouds, rain should happen. These are examples of imitative or memetic magic.

8. Religious practitioners

Almost all societies have part-time or full-time religious or magical practitioners. There are four major types of practitioners: shamans, sorcerers or witches, mediums, and priests.

A shaman is a religious intermediary, usually part-time, whose primary function is to cure people through sacred songs, pantomime, and other means; he is sometimes called a witch doctor by Westerners. He has a fairly high status in the society. He deals with the spirits to try to get their help or to keep them from causing harm.

The shaman enters into a trance, or some other altered state of consciousness, and then journeys to other worlds to get help from the guardians or other spirits. People may seek help through a shaman for practical matters. The shamans may also bring news from the spirits, such as a warning about an impending disaster.

Who becomes a shaman? Someone may receive a 'call' to become a shaman while recovering from an illness, or it may happen in a dream. Shamans in training may enhance the vividness of their trance experiences by using hallucinogens, by sleep or food deprivation, or by engaging in extensive physical activity such as dancing. Shamanistic training can take several years under the guidance of the master shaman.

Sorcerers and witches, unlike shamans, tend to have a very low social status. **Sorcery** refers to the use of certain materials to invoke supernatural powers to harm people. **Witchcraft** refers to the practice of attempting to harm people by supernatural means, but through emotions and thought alone, not through the use of any tangible objects. Suspected sorcerers and witches are usually feared. They may even be killed.

Mediums refer to part-time religious practitioners who are asked to heal and divine while in a trance. Mediums tend to be females. They are thought to be able to become possessed by spirits. Mediums are described as having tremors, convulsions, seizures and temporary amnesia during and after their trance states.

Priests are generally full-time specialists, with very high status, who are thought to be able to relate to superior or high gods beyond the ordinary person's access or control. They are often distinguished with special clothing. The training of a priest can be rigorous. Priests in India come from the Brahmin caste. If a shaman repeatedly fails to bring a cure, he may lose his following – a priest however has no such issue.

The more complex a society is, the more specialised practitioners it has. If a society has only one practitioner, it is almost always a shaman. That society tends to be that of nomadic or semi-nomadic foragers. Complex societies with classes usually have all the four types of practitioners.

9. Saora Shamans

Verrier Elwin (1955) gives an account of the shamans among the Saora of Southern Odisha in India. In a Saora village, the Kuranmaran or the shaman is the most important figure. He is believed to have the power to diagnose the source of a bodily or other trouble and also to cure or resolve it. His primary means is divination. In case of sickness, he seeks the cause in a trance or a dream. Every shaman has a tutelary wife in the underworld and she comes to assist him. If he is adept enough, he may go to other villages too.

The shaman's trance occurs in a ceremony in which the spirits are invited to be present. A ghost may come to instruct regarding something, may demand a sacrifice or warn about an epidemic. Visitors drop in to consult the shaman when he is in trance. Sometimes trances are spontaneous and sometimes induced. The shaman becomes whichever spirit that possesses him. Within an hour, he may play different parts. He weeps, laughs, and curses. He can become a woman, he can become an old person. A bargain also takes place between the spirits and the people. Different ghosts keep coming and going, sometimes without completing what they are saying. They can be talking normally, or be abusive and complaining. They would drink or eat, all through the shaman. A lot of conversations are about food and drink.

On one occasion, a ghost through the shaman demanded a particular type of woman, for sexual intercourse. A shanamin threw her arms around two men as a token of friendship. The scandals that no living person would dare talk about would be mentioned. When a widow fell ill once, her husband came laughing through the shaman and said, 'I had a fine time with her. She was going to marry someone, but I got her!' The shaman was told, 'Now draw an ikon showing what I did with her.' The shaman had to paint an image of copulation.

After the trance, the shaman often quietly passes out and spends the rest of the day asleep. Most shamans do not remember what they did in trance. A shaman must have a grasp of theology, geography, history, economics and genealogies. There is a lessening of inhibitions during the conversations with shaman and it has a healing effect.

Terms

1. **Religion:** any set of attitudes, beliefs and practices pertaining to supernatural power, whether that power rests in forces, gods, spirits, ghosts or demons.

2. **Supernatural:**powers believed to be not human or not subject to the laws of nature.

3. **Monotheistic:**believing that there is only one god and that all other supernatural beings are subordinate to, or are alternative manifestations of this supreme being.

4. **Polytheistic:**recognising many gods, none of whom is believed to be superordinate.

5. Animism:a belief in dual existence for all things – a physical, visible body, and a psychic, invisible soul.

6. Animatism:a belief in supernatural forces.

7. Mana:a supernatural, impersonal force that inhabits certain objects or people and is believed to confer success and/or strength.

8. Ghosts:supernatural beings who were once human; the souls of dead people.

9. Spirits:unnamed supernatural beings of nonhuman origin we are beneath the gods in prestige and often closer to the people; maybe helpful, mischievous or evil.

10. Divination:getting the supernatural to provide guidance.

11. Magic:the performance of certain rituals that are believed to compel the supernatural powers to act in particular ways.

12. Rituals:repetitive sets of behavior that occur in essentially the same patterns every time they occur. Religious rituals involve the supernatural in some way.

13. Sorcery:the use of certain materials to invoke supernatural powers to harm people.

14. Witchcraft:the practice of attempting to harm people by supernatural means, but through emotions and thought alone, not through the use of tangible objects.

15. Shaman:a religious intermediary, usually part-time, whose primary function is to cure people through sacred songs, pantomime, and other means; sometimes called witch doctor by Westerners.

16. Mediums:part-time religious practitioners who are asked to heal and divine while in a trance.

17. Priests:generally full-time specialists, with very high status, who are thought to be able to relate to superior or high gods beyond the ordinary person's access or control.

Think on it

1. How is religion defined?

2. Is religion a universal phenomenon?

3. Is man only rational? Should he be so?

4. Does the non-rationality of man contribute to religion?

5. What is the role of religion in explaining things?

6. What is animism? Explain.

7. How is animatism different from animism? Explain.

8. Is the religion of early Vedic period an example of naturism?

9. How is a fetish different from an amulet or an idol?

10. Explain fetishism.

11. Do all cultures fear ghosts? Explain.

12. Is there more distance between the people and their gods in modern societies? Is this an aspect of social change?

13. List the differences between religion and magic.

14. Can magic be used for good?

15. What is the difference between witchcraft and sorcery?

16. What happens to religion, magic and science as societies become modernised?

17. How is imitative magic different from contagious magic?

18. How is a priest different from a shaman?

19. Who is a medium?

20. Describe Shamanism in an Indian tribe.

CHAPTER TWENTY-ONE

Approaches to Religion

Founding a religion is not the same thing as following an already existing religion. Animism was not founded by anybody, animatism was not too. What happened in the last few millennia is that some people have succeeded in founding certain religions. They are now called the world religions. When we refer to religions, we normally mean these world religions: Islam, Judaism, Christianity, Buddhism, and Hinduism. Of these world religions, which is a religion that was not founded by anybody? Hinduism was not founded by anybody, but the other religions have founding figures. Complex societies have these world religions. Simple societies have tribal religions like animism, animatism, naturism, and ancestral worship.

1. Evolutionary approach

The evolutionary approach to religion refers to exploring how religion evolved from its earliest forms. E. B. Tylor proposed that animism was the earliest religion. Souls began to be associated with animals, trees, and pebbles, which gave rise to fetishism. Thereafter, specific spirits and gods began to be worshipped, which gave rise to polytheism. Polytheism later evolved into monotheism. Tylor was a Christian and Christianity is monotheistic and he thought his religion was the final and the last form of religion. But it is not necessary for us to agree that monotheism is the end point of religious evolution.

R.R. Marett proposed that animatism came earlier than animism. Marett modified Tylor's theory after he learnt of the belief in Mana among the Melanesians.

Emile Durkheim proposed that totemism was the earliest religion. He thought that Australian Aborigines were the most primitive people of the world, and their religion is totemism. Totemism refers to the worship of a totem and the rituals associated with it. Every clan has its own totem.

2. *Functional approach*

There are some people who worked on what may be regarded as the functions of religion. What is the function that a religion may be serving? It serves a psychological function. Religion answers certain questions. It may posit a purpose to life, it may give spiritual guidance. Such an approach to religion is called the psychological approach.

Some attributed social functions to religion. Social function means looking at what social purpose a religion is serving? The difference between a psychological function and a social function is that the former is about the individual and that latter is about the society. If you say that religion is serving some individual needs, then you are explaining it in psychological terms. If you are saying that this is how the society is being served by religion, then that is a social function. Durkheim and Marx wrote on the social functions of religion.

Malinowski explained that the religion of the Trobriand Islanders alleviated the stress in the individuals. Certain rituals were performed before the people set out on expeditions. These rituals were meant to seek the help of the supernatural for the successful outcome of an expedition. They reduced the anxiety.

Radcliffe Brown explained the social functions of religion. The supernatural elements punish the violation of the norms, and they approve the adherence to the norms. Thus religion contributes to survival of the society.

3. Durkheim on religion

Durkheim proposed that religion was not merely a matter of superstition. It is not opposed to science. Religion, to Durkheim, forms the identity of a group. People are divided into groups in a society, and a religion becomes the identity of a group. How did he get this idea? In his study of the Australian Aborigines, he saw that their society was divided into clans. Each clan had a totem, and there were practices associated with the totem; there were taboos and rituals. And he observed that they meant so much to the group. A clan is exogamous, a clan has political functions and economic functions. Durkheim understood that a totem was to a clan what a flag is to a nation.

The implication of the idea that religion serves as an identity is that even if one proves that religion is merely a superstition, it does not erode its significance much. If you take the Indian flag and use it to stitch pants, then it will be regarded as disrespecting the flag. On the other hand, if you use the same colors in a different way, say, in a vertical way, and make it into pants, it is not disrespectful. Why using the flag in that way is considered as disrespecting the nation? Because behind the flag there are the people, there is India. Disrespecting the flag means disrespecting the people. It symbolises the identity of India. Doing anything inappropriate to the national flag means offending India.

Similarly, disrespecting the Quran is offending the Muslims and desecrating a Hindu temple is offending all the Hindus. Those acts are offensive because those things symbolise the group. It is not related to logic. For example, when you enter the temple you have to leave your footwear outside. However, can you argue with the temple authorities, "The rule came because footwear is likely to be dirty, but I have brought new shoes and I am opening them now, can I go inside with these shoes?" No. The custom of leaving the footwear outside might have started because they carry dirt, that may be the origin, but now it has become a part of the rituals. Even if you say they are clean, you are violating the sanctity of the temple if you wear them inside. And when you are violating a ritual, you are violating an identity, you are violating a group. It is not strictly a logical thing. This means that a religion or a ritual have become identities. They become what Durkheim called 'sacred'.

To put it differently, the part of the society that assumes sacredness in relation to the society is what religion is. The source of that sacredness is the fact that the identity of the society is embedded in it. Why is the national flag sacred? Not because of the cloth, not because of any color intrinsically, but because a nation has chosen that as its identity. It means the identity of India is embedded in it. Religion serves the function of providing an identity to a group. This is so even in a multi-religious nation.

Look at this identity mechanism. Thinking of religion as an identity will help us understand certain things. For example, in Europe there has been a proposal to ban external religious symbols. And there is a proposal that Muslim women should not be allowed to wear the veil in public. and they said not wearing the veil in public would contribute to the freedom of the women. But the Muslim women went against it and said, 'We have a right to wear the veil, how can you force this rule on us?' Many people though do not understand what is meant by the right to wear a veil. Is it a matter of right to be unfree? Now, what is the issue involved here? Why might the Muslim women resist becoming more normal, more free? It is because the veil is a part of their identity. This is not about logic.

The part of the culture with which the identity is associated becomes sacred, and that is religion. The part with which the identity is not associated remains profane.

4. Marx on religion

Karl Marx was one person who was not fooled by religion. He knew that religion was a kind of a great game. Marx did not think that religion contained truth or wisdom. He did not believe that people should be religious. He thought, like Durkheim, that religion only serves a social function. And what is the social function it serves? He thought religion is used by the upper classes to dominate the lower classes.

To Marx, the society consists of the base and the superstructure. Technology and economy constitute the base. Religion is a part of the superstructure. The base influences the superstructure. The various classes in a society are part of the base. Particular beliefs are created for the higher classes to control the lower classes.

In the Hindu scriptures, who wrote the origin of varnas that describes how the Brahmins came about and how the Shudras came about? It was written by the Brahmins, the people who dominate. And they wrote it in such a way as to exalt themselves and degrade the Shudras. Religion is part of an elaborate manipulation system. The purpose of it is to perpetuate domination.

Why should the less-privileged believe in the religion? For them, religion offers hope that justice will be done in the end. To the masses, it is like the opium. Like a drug addict does not tackle a problem of his life and escapes from it, people do not address the issue of class conflict and take to religion, thereby escaping from dealing with class domination. The religion makes them think: this world is harsh, but after death my situation is going to be different; the people who are punishing me now will be punished later; and I am going to be rewarded later.

Religion gives a moral code, and that moral code is usually on the side of the dominant. For example, stealing is sinful in our societies, but hoarding and accumulation are not. Accumulation is glorified, but stealing is punished. And religion says, if you are not punished here, if the state fails to punish you here, there is the hell above.

If the Hindus behave properly in this world, then they will have a lot of dance programs to watch in the heaven. Rambha, Urvasi, Menaka. The untouchables should not question the system. And if they do as per the caste dharma, they will get those free tickets to the heaven. On the other hand, if they don't perform their dharma here, then they may go to the hell. What does this show? It shows that the basic moral code itself is a result of manipulation. Marx thinks that the moral code is manipulated. The moral code itself is not rational, it is not helpful for all,.

Think on it

1. What is Tylor's theory of evolution of religion?

2. What modification did Marett make to Tylor's theory?

3. What according to Malinowski are the functions of religion?

4. What is the psychological approach to religion?

5. What according to Radcliffe Brown are the functions of religion?

6. What is Durkheim's approach to religion?

7. How useful is Durkheim's theory in understanding conflict between religious groups?

8. What is Marx's approach to religion?

9. What is Marx's view on the moral code of a society?

10. Can Marx's approach to religion help us understand some elements of Hinduism?

CHAPTER TWENTY-TWO

Reflections on Religion

1. Founding of new religions

Let us examine how religions are founded. A person is teaching some deep things, people are listening; in time, many people may follow him, listen to him, admire him, but when can you say that now he has started his own religion? When can you say that he is no longer only a teacher or a preacher but a founder of a new religion?

Historically, it would seem that some people could start religions even though they did not want any such thing, and some others failed to start a religion though they tried hard to do it. Kabir was a very wise person and was very influential, but no religion was formed on the basis of his teachings. In the case of Nanak, however, a religion was formed on the basis of his teachings. Nanak did not want to create any new religion, but he ended up creating one. There was one person with great power who tried very hard to create a religion but couldn't. He was the great emperor Akbar. He tried hard, but the religion he started didn't spread. Prophet Mohammed created a religion. He knew what he was doing. And Jesus Christ probably did not want to create a religion, but he ended up creating one.

Sikhism was a strange case. Guru Nanak (1469-1539) thought: Hindus and Muslims are quarreling with each other, while God belongs to all. Nanak only talked about how God does not create divisions, these divisions are artificial, so in the eyes of God there are no Hindus and Muslims, and all are one. That's what he started teaching. The Hindus listened and the Muslims also listened, and Nanak thought he was bringing something which would create harmony between these two religions. And he said that somebody else would talk about it after he was gone. Then came the second Guru, and then the third. Ten Gurus came in succession. And at one stage, one of these Gurus, the fifth one, picked up a big fight with the Moghul emperor and was killed. The followers of the Guru made the Moghuls enemies. It was the 10[th]Guru, in 1699, who gave some external dress code to the initiates, which included uncut hair and sword. A distinct religion was thus born within a span of 150 years.

What was the original mission of Guru Nanak? Not to let disputes happen between religions, not to let the world be divided into religious groups. What happened by the time of the tenth Guru? The followers of Guru Nanak themselves became a distinct group. Instead of settling disputes between the two main religious groups, they themselves became another religious group, they fought with the Muslims first and later with the Hindus. In recent decades, this created so much violence – be it secessionism and terrorism.

For the Sikhs to go back to the original message of Guru Nanak, what should they do? They would have to forget all the divisions, including Sikhism. Guru Nanak stood for the dissolution of all divisions between people.

Let's come back to my question: When will a religious teacher become a founder of a new religion? If some people believe that what the teacher is saying is right, then would a religion start from him? In such a case, people might have believed that many things that Socrates was saying were true, but no religion was formed on the basis of Socratic teachings. Many people read Tukaram, many people read Kabir, but the followers of these Hindu saints didn't create any new religions.

Could one start a religion by claiming supernatural things? But Guru Nanak did not claim any supernatural thing, that he was the

Son of God or that he was a messenger. In fact, the Buddha also did not make any such claim. Only Prophet Mohammed and Jesus Christ made such claims. Will spiritual enlightenment of a teacher help him in creating a new religion? The Buddha was an enlightened person, he could create a religion. But Ramana Maharshi too was seen as an enlightened person, he didn't create any religion though. If a person is enlightened, people go and listen to him, and try to follow his teachings. That may be all.

It appears that when following a teaching, some people come to think that they are a distinct group, and then a religion could arise, as in the case of Sikhism. What is a religion? Truth getting converted into a separate identity. When we think 'We are Sikhs', a new religion is created. 'We are Christians', Christianity is created. 'We are Muslims', Islam is created. As long as you are thinking only that the teacher is saying something wise and you are trying to follow it, a new religion is not created. But when you think on the lines of 'I am a Muslim, my wife is also a Muslim, and our child is also going to be a Muslim', then there is religion. If your child is obviously going to be a Muslim, then you are part of the religion of Islam. On the other hand, if you think, "I like this master's teaching, my wife also may like it, but I don't know about my child," then it is not a religion. It is truth. It is influence.

Do you follow Durkheim's insight? He understood that religion in the final analysis is identity – though he did not discuss the founding of new religions or the connection between truth and identity. So if a truth remains just as a truth, a religion cannot be created out of it. When a truth is converted into an identity system, then a religion is created. A religion also comes with a moral code, Involving a supernatural element. Religion is about something that is very deep. That is why the identity created by a religion goes very deep. We have a teacher, we have a book, we have some festivals like the Guru's birthday, then we form a group. Religion is ultimately about grouping. As long as people are interested only in seeking the truth, a religion cannot be created out of it.

If you are reading the Vedas because they may contain some truth, then it is not about any religion. But if you are reading the Vedas because they are your scriptures, then that is religion. The belief in a certain supernatural element plus the grouping around it makes it a religion. This is a source of divisions in the society. It also means that we shouldn't question founder of our religion, whatever he said must be infallible. Because if he is not that great, then what are we? What Prophet Mohammed said long ago must be more relevant now. Our Vedas said things which are so profound, all modern science was already there in them. Why is it so? Because the Vedas are ours. That is how dogmatism is born – the attitude of 'how dare you say anything against our religion'.

When you criticise Socrates, you don't mean to be disrespectful to him. You think that's what he thought, given his times. You don't take a position that Socrates should always be right. You think he could be wrong too. Even if he was right then, he could be wrong now.

With identity, however, comes the dogmatism, the rigidity and taking criticism as a personal offence. In this process, people forget the truth. Guru Nanak might have said not to create divisions; but the followers ignored that and created a division.

J. Krishnamurti narrates an insightful story. A sage was touring the villages discussing the truth. Villagers gathered to listen to him. Watching this, a young devil was alarmed. As it did not want the truth to spread, it wanted to kill the sage. It consulted a senior devil to discuss its plans. What it heard from the senior devil was shocking: "Never kill a sage. Pick up those pieces of truth from what he utters. Make a book of them. That will become a sacred book. There would be people to interpret it, worship it, defend it and kill others in defense of it. A new religion would be born with all the dogmas. That would finish the truth. This is how we have been handling the problem of truth all along."

Given this situation, what should we be doing? Do we want religions? Should we create new religions? What do we do with these existing ones?

Questioning religion will mean questioning everything. And that would be the foundation of true freedom. Freedom should begin with disobeying the gods. 'The scripture says it, but I need not follow it. If there is some truth in something, I will follow it. If there is none, I will not. I will explore things for myself.' That should be the attitude towards religion.

2. Religion and education

Our education wants you to question many things, but it does not want you to question religion. It wants you to think, but think only in science and maths. If you want to think about the Vedas and the gods, it may be considered dangerous. People wouldn't know with what conclusions you may come up. This is not true education. True education should enable freedom, freedom in many ways.

Have you ever thought what all this education put together is about? Ultimately it only wants you to produce goods and services and contribute to the GDP. What is the IT sector for? Production and services. Electrical engineering, mechanical engineering – for production. MBA – to coordinate production and distribution. Do you ever ask: what is all this production for, why should we produce so much?

But you should start questioning. You should question: How should we lead life? In the present education, the bigger questions are not asked. You are asked to put all your energies on a very narrow spectrum of knowledge in order to make a livelihood.

One should be completely free. One should be free to explore: What is the soul? What is birth? Is there something like rebirth? What is God? How should I be related to God, if there is one? Why am I born? How should I live? It should not be like all the deeper questions of life are given some fixed answers and then you are asked to strive and succeed in life. Within that narrowly defined spectrum of life related to your chosen profession, you are asked to spend all your energy.

Religion also involves raising some fundamental questions. A political party may be involved simply in getting power, a company may be involved only in production and sales, but what does religion do? Religion asks some very basic questions, such as what is life for.

If you ask me why religion is surviving, it is because our education system doesn't let us ask these questions. If the basic questions were asked in the process of education, then religions won't have the power they have today. Because students will ask the fundamental questions and they will seek their own answers.

At present, the education we get is not letting us think about the fundamental questions of life. You have been studying and studying, did any textbook pose the question about the meaning of life? Or did any book you read ask you what you want to do with your life? Probably not.

The maximum issue raised, in something like sociology, is this: if you are at a lower level, if you are underprivileged, then how to be like the person at a higher level? As if the person at a higher level is enjoying the life so much. There are movements for the empowerment of the lower castes, empowerment of women, and so on. Indeed, if the men were so much in ecstasy, then the women should emulate them, but patently the men are not in ecstasy, so what are the women going to gain by copying them?

The questioning framework that we are taught is very narrow. When people read a certain scripture that is asking some deeper questions, they may suddenly realise, "Oh my God, I missed all this." They then go to a Swamiji with a long beard and say, "I have become successful in life, but my soul is poor, please guide me!" Had these people read the Vedas or other scriptures just the way they read science, then they would not be fooled by the length of the beard of the swamiji. Religions are surviving because of the narrowness of our education.

Old science is constantly being replaced by new science. In the same way, the old religion need not go on any longer, the old religions should be replaced by the new ones. There should be a different religion for the 21stcentury, by the 22ndcentury, it should be a different religion again.

Introduce the religious texts in the academic education. At first, the Hindus will criticise the Quran, and the Muslims will criticise the Gita. But after some time, all will lose their faith in their own scriptures. Finished. Then something new can be born.

The young men and women will be able to tell their parents, 'This is what you believe in, but it is not true'. When we break away from the past, a new beginning is possible. That's how we will get rid of all the outdated things in the society and that is the only way to create a new society.

Education should be a source of rupture between the old and the new. Children should not be taught as per the prejudices of their parents. They should be like Prahlada, who learnt about the true god by going against his own father. Education should create new ideas and new beliefs and lead us towards a new society.

Think on it

1. What do you know about how Guru Nanak founded a religion?

2. Is identity central to the religions as we know them today?

3. What are the consequences of truth becoming an identity?

4. What kind of people may have talent to found a religion?

5. Should education include the study of religious scriptures? Why so?

6. Should religions be updated just the way science textbooks are? What are your views?

7. Do you think present education is too narrow? Explain.

8. Is questioning religion helpful to a society? Explain.

Movie Review: The Man from Earth

The Man from Earth is a 2007 American science fiction film directed by Richard Schenkman.

Professor John Oldman (David Lee Smith) has quit his university job, after having worked there for 10 years, and is packing his things to move away. When his colleagues get to know this, they come to see him off. But they do not understand why he is leaving when he has been doing so well. John does not tell them the reason nor does he tell them anything about where he is going.

His colleagues notice some historical artifacts and paintings in his belongings and ask him about them. They see a burin that belongs to the Upper Paleolithic Age and get curious about it. Suddenly John asks them if it is possible for someone from the Upper Paleolithic, about 14,000 years ago, to survive till the present day. The biology professor answers that it is theoretically possible if cell replication takes place with exact copies; the appearance of the Paleolithic man too would be indistinguishable from that of a modern man and so would his intelligence.

While discussing about the Upper Paleolithic age, John begins to talk as if he himself lived in it, to the puzzlement of the people around. He begins to narrate how the earth changed. His learned colleagues pose him questions, trying to spot mistakes in his narrative.

A kind of a game ensues. John is assumed to be the man from the Upper Paleolithic. He goes on narrating what he has lived through all the millennia – the sweeping changes in human culture, civilization, technology, language, religion and other things as well as in global climate and geography. And his colleagues who come from various fields such as anthropology, archaeology, psychology and art history are expected to find fault in his narrative.

John narrates his story, what all he experienced and went through, as well as what he read about the ages he had witnessed. He would always try to correlate his memory with what he read in books. He was constantly learning all his extremely long life, and in the more modern times, he obtained doctorates in many subjects, working as a professor in many subjects.

Things become more intriguing and challenging when all the professors present fail to identify any mistake in a story based on such a preposterous claim. They start asking him some personal questions about things like how the others were treating him seeing that he was not aging at all, and whether there were others like him. He talks about the problems he faced in the beginning, how for a long time he did not realize he was different. He tells them he found it safe to move to some new place every ten years, which is what he is doing now too.

John also drops the names of some famous personalities he met over the course of so many centuries. He sailed with Columbus once. Van Gogh was his friend and gave him his painting. When he had free time, he would go to New Guinea where he was worshipped as a deity.

Then the conversation turns to religion. John says he was in India when Buddha was alive and he was a disciple of Buddha. Buddha did sense John was different in some way but did not know what it was. John stayed with Buddha till the end.

Then his colleagues get curious to know if John met any important personalities from the Bible. John is reluctant to talk at first, but then opens up . Some 500 years after Buddha's death, he wanted to go to the Roman Empire, which was then a killing machine, to preach Buddhism. But he could not stand up against the empire.

His colleagues are shocked when John says that the legend of Jesus Christ was born from him. He tells them that much of the Bible is fiction. He did not perform any miracles like walking on the water or raising the dead. He did some healing with the Eastern medicine that he had learnt. Was the resurrection true? John says he blocked out the pain during the crucifixion, in which he was only bound to a pole and not nailed to it. He could bring down the life processes in his body to an undetectable level. He learnt these yogic techniques while he was in India and Tibet. So when they thought he was dead, they put him in a cave. He became normal and wanted to go his own way, but some of his followers saw him and did not listen to what he was trying to say

John says he never said he was the son of God, he only said he had a master greater than him. He did not talk about any heaven except about the goodness on earth. Regarding the Sermon on the Mount, he says that he does not remember what he said except that one day he taught on a hill and not many people stayed to listen to him.

Edith, a professor of art history and a devout Christian, is shocked and confused. She has an emotional breakdown and starts crying. Will, a psychiatry professor who has been very skeptical of John's narrative coerces him to admit that his whole claim is a hoax. John accepts that it is all a prank. All except Will and Sandy, a professor of history, leave with varying degrees of belief in John's story.

Sandy, who has been in one-sided love with John, trusts the entire story, and asks him questions about his previous names. While John gives Sandy a list of some of his more recent names, Will, the sixty year old psychiatry professor, recognizes the name of his biological father who abandoned the family. He then asks John some questions which only a close family member could answer, and he does. John's entire story could after all be very much true.

Books Followed

The following works have been consulted while writing this book:

1. *Cultural Anthropology* (14th edition) by Ember & Ember
2. *Cultural Anthropology* (6th edition) by Marvin Harris & Orna Johnson
3. *Social Anthropology* by Majumdar & Madan
4. *Family, Kinship and Marriage in India* edited by Patricia Uberoi
5. *Sociology: Themes and Perspectives* (8th edition) by Haralambos & Holborn [for methods]
6. *Sociological Theory* (8th edition) by George Ritzer [for feminism]
7. *Religion in India* edited by T.N. Madan [for shamanism]
8. *The Evolution of Desire* by David M. Buss [for evolutionary psychology]